How to a Clinical Psycholog

D0659414

Based on information gathered from assistant psychologists, trainee clinical psychologists and clinical psychology course directors across the country, *How to Become a Clinical Psychologist* includes:

- information on work experience
- advice on job applications and interviews
- details of research projects and training
- guest chapters dealing with professional issues

This guide is the first of its kind and will be an essential companion for anyone interested in pursuing a career in clinical psychology.

Alice Knight is currently training on the doctoral programme in clinical psychology at the University of Manchester. Prior to this she worked as an assistant psychologist and research assistant within the NHS.

WITHDRAWN BY THE
UNIVERSITY OF MICHIGAN

How to Become a Clinical Psychologist

GETTING A FOOT IN THE DOOR

Alice Knight

FOREWORD BY GRAHAM TURPIN

Brunner-Routledge
Taylor & Francis Group

HOVE AND NEW YORK

UGL
RC
467.95
.K55
2002

First published 2002 by Brunner-Routledge
27 Church Road, Hove, East Sussex, BN3 2FA

Simultaneously published in the USA and Canada
by Brunner-Routledge
29 West 35th Street, New York, NY 10001

Brunner-Routledge is an imprint of the Taylor & Francis Group

© 2002 Alice Knight

Typeset in Lucida Casual and Benguiat Frisky
by Keystroke, Jacaranda Lodge, Wolverhampton
Printed and bound in Great Britain
TJ International, Padstow, Cornwall
Cover design by Richard Massing

All rights reserved. No part of this book may be reprinted or
reproduced or utilised in any form or by any electronic, mechanical,
or other means, now known or hereafter invented, including
photocopying and recording, or in any information storage or
retrieval system, without permission in writing from the publishers.

British Library Cataloguing in Publication Data
A catalogue record for this book is available from the British Library

ISBN 1-58391-242-8

ug1
42157158
ug1
7-2-03

FOR MY PARENTS WITH LOVE AND
THANKS

Contents

Foreword

There is an increasing demand within health and social services for well-trained applied psychologists who are able to offer individualised therapy, to advise and train other staff, to empower organisations and to audit and research. Clinical psychology as a profession has been offering many of these skills and has grown exponentially to meet this demand over the last couple of decades. Fortunately, psychology is one of the most popular subjects read at degree level within the UK and this ensures that there is also an ever-increasing supply of graduate psychologists wishing to use their psychology in real world settings.

Although the developments and growth in the profession highlighted above are to be welcomed and embraced wholeheartedly, the pressure and competition to gain postgraduate training in applied psychology is immense. Having sat on interview panels for clinical psychology training courses over the last twenty years, I am always struck by the sheer determination and initiative of many of the graduates seeking to gain a training place. Similarly, there are always a number of application forms from what look to be really good applicants who have not adequately attended to the form, presumably not knowing the degree of competition or having been poorly advised. Accordingly, as a trainer I welcome the arrival of this book. I hope it will help both assistants and the services that employ them to become clearer about the assistant role and the responsibilities of the employer. With assistant psychologists becoming increasingly valued I suspect there will come a time when their role will become a recognised and appropriately trained part of the workforce assisting in delivering psychological services on a regular and permanent basis.

Before we get to such a development, it is important to recognise that the profession has a responsibility to its graduate psychologists in supporting their efforts to gain a place within postgraduate training courses. This book will significantly help the provision of much-needed advice and support. It is well informed, well researched, and clearly and sensibly written. For people wishing to pursue a career as an assistant or clinical psychologist, the book offers invaluable advice on preparing for and gaining a place both as an assistant and also as a trainee clinical psychologist. Although preparation is important, as an interviewer for clinical courses you also need to remember that sometimes you can become over rehearsed. Remember it is important to think about and answer the question that has been asked of you, rather than offer the answer that you prepared earlier! Try to be calm, reflective and, above all, yourself.

Finally, on behalf of the Group of Trainers in Clinical Psychology, I would like to wish anyone reading this book good luck in their future careers and I look forward to welcoming you later on into the profession.

Professor Graham Turpin
Chair of the Group of Trainers in Clinical Psychology and Director of the North Trent/University of Sheffield Doctorate in Clinical Psychology.

Preface

I graduated with a degree in psychology in 1998 not knowing exactly what I wanted to do with it. After a few difficult months of exploring my interests and options I decided to pursue a career in clinical psychology. At this stage I came across a problem - how should I go about doing this? I did not know anybody who worked within this field or anybody else with a similar interest to me. I spent a lot of time trying out different ways of getting information but with very little luck. After writing to a number of clinical psychologists in the area I managed to get some voluntary work experience in a clinical psychology department working alongside some research assistants on a research project. A few months later I secured my first assistant psychologist post. I had gathered a lot of information from the various routes I had explored and subsequently learnt a great deal more from the other assistant psychologists I had met. The paths they had taken to get their posts followed a similar route to mine and I realised that I had not been alone in my difficulties. I reflected that, 'If only I knew then what I know now, it would have saved me a lot of time and heartache'. This is what inspired me to put this book together. I have been working on it over the past two years whilst I worked as an assistant and more recently as a trainee. Over time its development has been greatly influenced by the advice that I have been given from numerous people within the profession to whom I am extremely grateful. I hope you find it useful and good luck in your career!

Abbreviations

BPS	British Psychological Society
DCP	Division of Clinical Psychology
NHS	National Health Service
Clin.Psy.D Course	Clinical Psychology Doctorate Course

Acknowledgements

I would like to thank all the people below for their part in helping me put this book together:

Linda Steen, who very kindly supervised me throughout the researching and writing of this book. She has been extremely supportive and helped to keep me motivated. Her input has had a significant influence on the progress of the book at each stage of its development and her advice has been invaluable.

Will, my brother, for all his help in making this book look more appealing, and certainly more amusing, with his illustrations. His talent and dedication have always inspired me.

Graham Turpin, for kindly writing the foreword to this book and providing positive feedback.

Guest authors Chris Hatton, Anna Phillips and Ian Gray for contributing a chapter about the research they have been carrying out with the clearing house. The current members of the DCP Affiliates Group for contributing a guest chapter about the DCP. They include Emmett Maher, Angharad Rudkin, Peter Corr, Becky Goody, Catherine O'Callaghan, Jane Nye, Ruppert Noad, Mags Spendlove and Lindsey Hume.

The participants, without whom it would not have been possible. They include Elizabeth Adey, Katherine Allen, Debbie Allen, Kate Allez, Vicki Ashton, Neil Austen, Rachel Avande, Charlotte Baker, Elina Baker, Sarah Bates, Nicola Belsham, Tracy Belshaw, Richard Bennett, Esther Black, Jo Black, Kirsty Black, Angela Boggett, Emily Boye, Corinna Broder, S. Brooke, Nicola Brown, Susan Brown, Abi Burridge, S. Burrows, Sarah

Butchard, Catherine Butler, Helen Cadman, Rachel Calam, Anna Carey, B. Carter, Phil Charlesworth, Gina Charlton, Jasmine Chin, Lisa Chyyill, Erica Clayton, Andrea Collins, Hazel Connery, Patricia Conway, Emma Cotes, Peter Corr, Jude Courtney, Jenni Crean, Calum Crosthwaite, R. Dawson, Cindy Davies, Teresa Deane, Catherine Derbyshire, Tim Devine, Corinne Dickson, Mathew Diver, Mhairi Donaldson, Ruth Drake, L. Durell, Katie Ann Elliot, Peter Elliott, Hannah Falvey, John Foa, Fiona Fraser, Ann Galloway, Heidi Gibbins, Kate Gillian, Sarah Gore, Fiona Grant, Lucy Grant, Joanne Green, Mary Grigg, R. Goodey, Patricia Hall, Vicky Hancock, Derek Hanlon, I. Hargreaves, Kate Harman, S. Harper, Becci Harris, Hilly Harvey, Andy Hawkins, Tracey Hever, Kerry Hill, Sarah Hill, Kate House, Paula Hull, Lloyd Humphreys, Kate Hunt, R. Hunter, Pamela Jarrie, Steve Jefferis, Joanna, Luke Jones, Menna Jones, Julia, Sylvia Kapp, Ruth Keenan, Wendy Kellaway, Sue Kellell, Elizabeth Kent, Tania Knight, Kirsty Lamb, Emma Lander, Anne Lane, Vicky Laute, Tony Lavender, Lisa Law, Jayne Levell, Joanne Little, Sue Llewelyn, Katy Lobley, Becky Lowe, Paul Lyons, Fiona MacDonald, Sophie Mackrell, Richard Madronal-Luque, Zoey Malphus, E. Maher, Kalli Mantala-bozos, Joanne Martin, Sarah Mayhead, Sophie Mayhew, M. McCulloch, Lynne McDonald, Tracey McElroy, Jean McFarlane, Zoe McGovern, S. McKeown, Nicola Meechan, Ayishah Meer, Tracey Millar, Ed Miller, James Millington, Derek Milne, Caroline Moffat, Steff Moulton, Stephen Mullin, Tara Murphy, Helen Nicolson, Karen Oaksford, Catherine O'Callaghan, B. O'Neill, John Owen, Louise Pearson, Jackie Peyton, Emma Prett, Ben Pumps, Lisa Rabone, Harriet Radermacher, Helen Reader, Hayler Richardson, Gemma Ridel, Liz Riley, Clare Roberts, Dave Robinson, K. Rooke, Sharon Roscoe, Jo Rowland, Paul Russell, Donna Saddlington, Kelly Sathananthan, P. Sargeaunt, Philippa Saul, Caroline Scott, Claire Seddon, Maureen Seils, Fiona Senior, Anita Sidlar, Cherry Smith, Kate Somerville, R. J. Stokoe, Helen Soper, Michael Stoker, Emily Street, Catherine Sugden, Claire Summerscales, Rachel Sweetingham, N. Symons, Lorraine Tatum, Jo Thomas, Nessa Thomas, Lisa Thorne, Joanne Timms, Karen Titley, Helen Toone, K. Townshend, Vanessa Trowell, Clare Trudgeon, Jillian Turner, Lara Walford, Jonathan Ward, Sarah Ward, Angela Watson, Charlotte Webb,

Michelle Webster, Matilda West, Nicky Weyman, Jo White, Lisa Whiteside, Lois Whittall, Amy Wicksteed, Jennifer Wiley, Nicola Wise, Merry Womphrey, Anita Wraith, Gayle Yeardley, and also those who wished to remain anonymous.

All those people who helped me along the way with regards to the researching, writing and publishing of this book. I would particularly like to thank Professor Nicholas Tarrier, Alison Marriott, Dr Tony Morrison, Dave Harper, Patrick Winegar, Christian Winegar, and Merope Mills.

My parents, Carolyn and Bill, for their support and encouragement in helping me get to this point; Lloyd for believing in me; and my cats, Timon and Pumba, for keeping me company at the computer.

1 | Introduction

The aim of this book is to offer information and advice for anyone interested in pursuing a career in clinical psychology. This information and advice has been gathered from assistant psychologists around the country based on their personal experiences of trying to get into the field of clinical psychology and of working as an assistant psychologist. It also incorporates some advice from current trainee clinical psychologists on different courses in Chapter 8 and from a number of course directors at the end of Chapter 6.

You will also find two guest chapters that enhance the information provided in the rest of the book. Chapter 7 reports on the initial findings from an ongoing research project relating to Clin.Psy.D course selection. These findings support the more qualitative information gathered in the rest of the book. Chapter 9 provides a detailed description of the Affiliates Group of the Division of Clinical Psychology (DCP) of the British Psychological Society (BPS). It explains how it could be a useful port of call for further information leading on from topics discussed in this book.

By combining these elements the overall purpose of this book is to act as a self-help text offering both support and practical advice by learning from the experiences of others. It is not intended as a direct guide to entering the profession. As one participant pointed out: 'there isn't a structure on how to get into clinical psychology like other careers such as law'. Another also highlighted that 'many people on the clinical courses have never been an assistant psychologist anyway' and that this is not the only route into clinical psychology, albeit the most popular. Another participant clarified this point by stating: 'there is no magic formula to getting on to clinical psychology training once you graduate from your undergraduate course'.

This is all worth bearing in mind when using this book. It does not provide 'the answer' but it should help you to find your own route into this profession if it is the appropriate profession for you. Therefore, overall this book aims to provide a good starting point to help guide people in the right directions and get 'a foot in the door'.

The book has been laid out to enable you to dip into the sections that you find relevant and useful for yourself at different stages. You will also find me popping up occasionally in cartoon form to help illustrate points and hopefully add a little humour.

THE QUESTIONNAIRES AND THE PARTICIPANTS

Three questionnaires were designed and sent to relevant participants across England, Scotland and Wales. Northern

Ireland and Eire operate their own system for training in this area but the information in this book is still likely to be useful for people there. One questionnaire was designed for assistant psychologists, one for trainee clinical psychologists and one for Clin.Psy.D course directors. Below is some information about the questionnaires and the participants.

Assistant psychologists

I was initially quite nervous about sharing this idea with fellow assistant psychologists, fearing a negative reaction, that it was in fact only me who thought this would be useful. However, I have in fact been delighted with the extremely positive feedback that I have received. I devised a questionnaire (see Appendix 1), which I sent to assistant psychologists across the country. I did this mainly through contacting various assistant psychologist groups, but I also put an advert in the British Psychological Society (BPS) monthly magazine *The Psychologist*, and in the monthly journal of the Division of Clinical Psychology (DCP) of the BPS, *Clinical Psychology* (previously known as *Clinical Psychology Forum*).

The questionnaire provided the opportunity for assistant psychologists to share their personal experiences to date of trying to pursue a career in clinical psychology and to give advice based on this. Each individual has obviously had different experiences and therefore advice did vary. As a result you may find at times that some advice is contradictory but this is reflective of the mixture of views that certain topics evoked. In order to deal with this I mainly tried to piece together the most useful pieces of information, much of which was repeated amongst many of the questionnaires. The contents of this book are set out within the general framework of this questionnaire with some important additions also included. It is therefore set around the information provided by the participants so it should be representative of their collective experiences and advice.

The response was tremendous and I received 124 completed questionnaires. With no national figures for the number of assistant psychologist posts it is unfortunately difficult to state what percentage of all assistant psychologists this reflects. The male:female ratio amongst the participants was 1:6. The average age of the participants was 26 years old (ranging from 21 to 46). Of the participants 51 per cent were in their first assistant psychologist post, 35 per cent were in their second, 11 per cent were in their third and 3 per cent were in their fourth. Based on my personal experience, these statistics appeared to be quite representative of the overall assistant psychologist population in the United Kingdom. There are however no statistics available for an accurate comparison to the overall population to be drawn.

Trainee clinical psychologists and course directors

As the writing of the book progressed I decided to send out two additional questionnaires in order to gather further useful information. The information gathered from them is represented solely in two of the chapters. Chapter 8 is dedicated to the responses gathered from current trainee clinical psychologists who completed the trainee questionnaire (see Appendix 2). This provides an opportunity for people at the next stage of their career path to reflect on their previous experience and give advice based on this.

Similarly, at the end of Chapter 6 there is some general advice gathered using a brief questionnaire (see Appendix 3) with a number of Clin.Psy.D course directors. This is in relation to the application process, which serves to enhance the advice provided by assistant psychologists that has been compiled within that chapter. Once again you may find that some of the information offered seems contradictory but I felt that it was important for me to include all angles presented in order for the information to remain as broad as possible. For more information on the outcome of both these questionnaires please consult the relevant chapters.

WHAT IS CLINICAL PSYCHOLOGY?

This question seemed to fill the participants with dread as it is asked on the application form for the Clin.Psy.D courses.

It is not as straightforward as it may appear, a fact reflected in the variety of answers provided in the questionnaires. The descriptions given did however follow some similar themes. These themes are also covered in the description below by Marzillier and Hall (1999) who defined the role of a clinical psychologist as follows:

Clinical psychologists are health care professionals who work in the fields of mental and physical health. Amongst their main activities are: (a) Psychological assessment, that is the use of psychological methods and principles to gain better understanding of psychological attributes and problems. The assessment of cognitive function (memory, intelligence, spatial abilities) following head injury, is one well-established example of psychological assessment. (b) Psychological treatment, that is the use of psychological procedures and principles to help others bring about change. There are many forms of psychological treatment, ranging from brief practical procedures for overcoming specific fears to lengthy and complex treatments such as some form of psychoanalysis. (c) Psychological evaluation, that is the use of psychological principles to evaluate the effectiveness of treatments or other forms of intervention. Clinical psychologists have been particularly involved in developing methods of evaluating psychotherapies and to a lesser extent physical forms of therapy.

Although these are the main activities of clinical psychologists, there are also others. Training of other professional staff, involvement in administration and advice, involvement in health service policies, and collaborative research are all activities that some clinical psychologists engage in as part of their work.

The important thing to note about the role of a clinical psychologist is that it is extremely varied and no one clinical psychologist does exactly the same job as another. As highlighted above, there are many different aspects of work that a clinical psychologist can get involved in and to differing degrees, with a variety of client groups and in a wide range of settings. The role of a clinical psychologist is also continuing to expand as the profession at large develops within the changing culture of the NHS. Therefore, there is no one 'role' of a clinical psychologist, but a number of roles, each carried out to varying degrees by individual clinical psychologists. When considering a career in clinical psychology it is therefore important to think about how appealing you would find these different roles, both individually and in combination. Below is a list of some of the roles that you may want to consider.

- ⊃ Psychological assessment and formulation with individuals, groups or carers
- ⊃ Therapeutic interventions with individuals, groups or carers and evaluation of outcome
- ⊃ Research with clients, carers, health professionals and 'normal' populations. This can be both theoretically and/or practically based and the aim is to aid in
- ⊃ improving both clinical practice and the theoretical base that it draws from
- ⊃ Audit of, for example, the effectiveness of psychological services
- ⊃ Consultation with other professionals
- ⊃ Teaching/training of both those within the profession and people in related health professions
- ⊃ Supervision within the profession and of other related health professionals
- ⊃ Involvement in health service policies
- ⊃ Management of services
- ⊃ Liaison as part of a multidisciplinary team
- ⊃ Administration
- ⊃ Promoting mental health issues and psychological services

WHAT IS THE ROLE OF AN ASSISTANT PSYCHOLOGIST?

As the name suggests, an assistant psychologist assists clinical psychologists in their work in some or all of the areas highlighted above. They usually do this under the supervision of a clinical psychologist, and like clinical psychologists, the role of an assistant psychologist varies from job to job. It should be noted that some assistant psychologist jobs do not involve working directly for a clinical psychologist but for other related professionals. Posts are usually from six months to a year long but some can be renewed. The Department of Health has also recently altered its guidance to allow assistant psychologists to be employed for longer than twelve months in one contract. There are standardised salary scales though you can start at different levels depending on your previous experience and the funding available. The experience gained as an assistant psychologist should provide an insight into the field of clinical psychology and the experience relevant for applying for clinical psychology training.

Often assistant psychologists carry out more than one post in order to gain a wider variety of experiences needed to apply for further training. These posts are not, however, solely viewed as opportunities to gain the relevant experience needed to apply for courses, but provide important input into the psychological work carried out in the NHS or in universities. Further information regarding the role of an assistant psychologist is provided in Chapter 5.

It is important to note that the nature of the work, quality of supervision and experience offered varies tremendously across posts. However, the Division of Clinical Psychology recently issued some updated guidelines for the employment of an assistant psychologist to which employers are supposed to adhere.

Assistant psychologists/research assistant psychologists

Please note that I will use the term 'assistant psychologist' throughout this text in reference to both the role of an 'assistant psychologist' and a 'research assistant psychologist'. Both assistant psychologists and research assistant psychologists completed the questionnaire and both jobs provide very useful, relevant experience in this field. The majority of participants were however, working as assistant psychologists and therefore there is a general leaning towards this direction in the information.

TRAINING TO BECOME A CLINICAL PSYCHOLOGIST

In order to become qualified as a clinical psychologist in the United Kingdom you must first gain a bachelor's degree in psychology (either a BSc or a BA) from a BPS approved course (one that allows you to gain a graduate basis for registration). This usually has to be an upper second class honours degree or above. It is still possible with a lower second class degree but you may find it helpful if you then did a postgraduate course as well (for example, a masters degree or a doctorate). This can sometimes be achieved as part of a job as an assistant psychologist. It is therefore worth enquiring about this. It is also worth enquiring about how lower degree classes are viewed, as this differs from course to course.

In addition to this you need some relevant work experience. There is no set amount of time or type of experience that you need to get; it varies for each person depending on a number of other factors (for example, the quality of experience, previous experiences, and the individual's personal qualities). The most common way of getting relevant work experience currently is through working alongside qualified clinical psychologists as an assistant psychologist for a few years (usually between one and four years). Prior to this you also usually need some experience in order to get an assistant psychologist post, as explained in Chapter 2. Alternatively to working as an assistant psychologist, there are a number of other routes that people have taken in related areas, usually through the kinds of experience covered in Chapter 2. The next step is to apply to a clinical psychology doctorate course, which lasts for three years. This provides both theoretical and practical experience within the various areas in which clinical psychologists work. Chapters 6 and 7 provide information about getting on to a clinical psychology training course. Successful completion of this course then allows you to practise as a qualified clinical psychologist in the National Health Service.

WHY CLINICAL PSYCHOLOGY?

When asked why they wanted to pursue a career in clinical psychology participants provided a number of reasons. The most popular reason involved a desire to work in a caring profession with people. In addition to this, various people noted their interest in working in mental health in this capacity because you can work with a range of client groups and professionals within a multidisciplinary setting, and get involved in services in a variety of capacities (for example, research, clinical, training, management etc.). It is widely viewed as a challenging yet flexible and rewarding profession. It is also seen to have good job prospects once you have completed the clinical psychology training and salaries are said to compare favourably to other psychology professions (for example, educational or academic psychology). Below is an example of an answer provided by one of the assistant psychologists who completed the questionnaire.

'It seemed to encompass the reasons that I took a degree in psychology in the first place. I wasn't interested in the best designs for an efficient kettle, or how supermarkets encourage you to buy certain products - I wanted to work with people with mental health problems. I also have a real interest in biological sciences but thought that I would find a lot of those courses a bit dry so I combined psychology with physiology, which was an ideal combination of my interests. I had thought about studying medicine but that seemed to be treating the body, not the person. Clinical psychology includes working with people, and working with medical conditions but more than that it involves an holistic approach where you are treating the whole person. I also like the fact that I do not have to sacrifice my scientific nature, psychology is a science but it also has room to be flexible. And lastly, I was excited by the prospect that psychology is a relatively new area with room to develop new ideas and theories, I liked the idea of being at the forefront of new discoveries.'

Another good reason given was that 'it beats entering 'Endurance' (a famously challenging Japanese competition); that's for wimps!'

GETTING FURTHER INFORMATION

There are a variety of sources from which people try to get information when they decide to seek a career in clinical psychology. The problem appears to be, however, that the sources offer limited information, which can also be contradictory, and sometimes completely wrong. A number of participants stated that they gradually gathered the necessary information through a process of trial and error, which was also my experience. This book has received a lot of positive feedback from assistant psychologists around the country who believed that a central reference would have been very useful and saved them a lot of time. This book does not intend to replace all other possible sources but aims to guide people in the appropriate direction to finding further information. Below are the main routes that participants took in search of information about this field and a summary of how useful they found them.

- Most people appear to have sought advice from within their university, by approaching both lecturers and careers departments. There were a number of complaints about adopting this strategy, however, because a lot of psychology undergraduate departments and careers services seem to have very little information and a commonly unhelpful message is that it is too competitive an area to be worth considering. The perspectives provided seem to depend largely on the individual that you contact.
- Contacting the BPS for general advice is another option and some people seem to have found this useful.
- Contacting the Affiliates Group of the DCP of the BPS could be useful. They have recently become increasingly involved in raising the profile of assistant psychologist issues and are compiling a number of resources that you may find useful. They also hold annual conferences that could be worth enquiring about. For further information see Chapter 7.
- The most popular way of getting useful information appears to have been through discussions with people who are already involved in this area: clinical psychologists, trainee psychologists and assistant psychologists. If you do not know anyone in this field then it is a good idea to be proactive in gaining some useful contacts.
- There is a book by Marzillier and Hall (1999) *What is Clinical Psychology?*, which provides a good description of the work that goes on in this area but not of how to get into it.
- There are assistant psychologist groups around the country that hold regular meetings and are a great source for learning more about clinical psychology, how to get into it, and the reality of working as an assistant psychologist. Assistant psychologist jobs are often mentioned at such meetings and guest speakers (usually clinical psychologists) are invited to present on a variety

of topics. The groups are run separately by assistant psychologists across the country so the best thing to do would be to contact your local group to find out exactly how they operate and how you could become involved. The Affiliates Group of the Division of Clinical Psychology (DCP) of the British Psychological Society (BPS) has a database of contact details for groups around the country (see Chapter 7).

- At the end of this book is a list of useful references which provide an insight into key issues relating to assistant psychologist work. A lot of them are articles from *Clinical Psychology* (previously *Clinical Psychology Forum*), the monthly journal produced by the DCP. To get hold of copies you should contact the DCP or ask around if anyone you know subscribes to it.

- Another great way to gain both contacts and a real taste of the area is to do some work experience (see Chapter 2).

2 | Work experience

WORK EXPERIENCE PRIOR TO GETTING AN ASSISTANT PSYCHOLOGIST POST

People appear to carry out a number of different jobs, both paid and voluntary, prior to gaining a post as an assistant psychologist. All work experience of any kind is obviously beneficial because it gives you a taste of what it is like to work in the 'real world'. However, certain kinds of experience appear to be more useful than others because they relate more to the work that you would carry out as a clinical psychologist. Below is a list of the kinds of work experience that a large number of people have found strengthened their application for assistant psychologist posts. This should help to steer you in the right direction when looking for appropriate work experience.

You can work with various client groups within the roles below. If you carry out a number of jobs it could help to enhance your curriculum vitae if you gain as much varied experience as possible with different client groups. This is not an exhaustive list so you may have some other good ideas too. Please note that the titles used also have other variations for the same job in different places. For further information regarding this kind of work there are useful addresses in Appendix 4 that you could use.

Support worker

You may find it easier to get a paid job as a support worker instead of a job as an assistant psychologist. Quite a few people carry out this kind of work for a while before getting an assistant psychologist's job. You will find such jobs available in a number of organisations. A good port of call initially would be local social services.

Nursing assistant psychologist

Some assistant psychologists have previously done nursing work. This can be done with a variety of client groups (including the mental health sector). To find out how to get involved in this kind of work you should contact hospitals in your area.

Care worker

For example, in day care centres, nursing homes or with individuals. This work can be done in a voluntary or paid capacity.

Assistant in special schools

There are a number of schools across the country that are specialised, for example, for children with emotional and behavioural difficulties or learning difficulties. They employ people to work as assistant psychologists in the classrooms or to work specifically with individuals, alongside other things.

Helpline volunteer

There are a number of charities that have helplines. You can also find helplines for university students that need volunteers (for example, Nightline). Working as a helpline volunteer provides the opportunity to develop communication skills that are always valuable within clinical psychology. Training is usually provided.

Lovaas therapist

There is a need for Lovaas therapists across the country. This involves working with children with autism in their own homes using behaviour modification therapy. You do not have to have any previous experience of the area because you get trained on the job, but you are generally required to have a degree in psychology.

Charities volunteer

There are various charities around the country that would be very grateful for volunteers. It could be useful to work for a charity that is involved either in mental health or with certain client groups with whom clinical psychologists work.

Volunteer at university

Many universities have a student voluntary service. You could enquire about voluntary activities that would provide relevant experience for you. Alternatively, most towns and cities have a volunteer bureau that may also offer relevant experience.

Camp counsellor

There are various schemes that offer the opportunity to work with children in summer camps (usually in North America).

Many people who get involved in these schemes also enjoy the chance to travel around the States once the camp has ended. These are often advertised at universities and you could enquire at career centres about this.

Working in clinical psychology departments

It can be a good idea to contact your local clinical psychology departments and send them your curriculum vitae and a covering letter stating who you are and why you would like to get some work experience. People have experienced a variety of outcomes through taking this approach. You may find that they offer you some work experience as a voluntary assistant psychologist or an opportunity to shadow somebody from the department. This gives you the chance to get a taste of what it is really like to work in this area and gives you a few contacts who may be able to offer useful advice. On the other hand they may not reply at all, or they may keep your details for the future or pass them on to another party who may be able to help. Whatever the outcome, this is certainly a useful approach to take. Some of the participants even ended up getting posts within departments that they had approached.

Working in undergraduate psychology departments

Some people carry out additional research work within their psychology department during their undergraduate course. This can be paid or voluntary, and can be carried out during term time or during the holidays. It can be very valuable experience which could help in getting you more work after you get your degree. It is worth enquiring about this kind of work as it is not necessarily advertised.

Undergraduate psychology placements

Some university courses can include a year of paid or unpaid work experience. Participants who had done a course like this were in favour of this option. It is something you may want to bear in mind if you are still deciding on which university to apply to. Morrison, Linger and Beck-Sanders (1999) wrote about their experiences of undergraduate psychology place- ments and stated that they found it beneficial and rewarding for both the students and the employer. They highlight, however, a few pitfalls that they came up against which would be worth considering if you are going to follow a similar route.

WHEN TO START GAINING RELEVANT EXPERIENCE

People completing the questionnaires started to gain relevant experience at various points depending on when they realised what they wanted to do and that experience was important. However, the advice passed on by the majority of people was to start looking for experience AS SOON AS POSSIBLE!!

As soon as you have started considering a career in this area it is worth doing some relevant work experience in order to get a taste of whether you would like working in this field. If you then decide that this profession is for you it is important to gain as much varied work experience as possible before trying to get on to the clinical psychology training courses or an assistant psychologist post. Remember that 'the early bird catches the worm'.

The majority of people advise that a good time to start gaining experience is during your undergraduate course, during term time or in the holidays if this is possible. However, it is important not to jeopardise your degree by doing this because good academic qualifications are crucial for getting on to a clinical psychology training course. One assistant psychologist pointed out that another benefit to doing some work experience during your undergraduate course could be that 'it also helps with your studies because it puts everything into a 'real world' context instead of it just being words on a page'. It is also important to remember to 'do something you enjoy'.

ADDITIONAL ADVICE FROM ASSISTANT PSYCHOLOGISTS

There was a lot of repetition in advice about how and where to look for relevant work experience. The most common advice was to write to clinical psychology departments with your curriculum vitae and a covering letter. Below are some additional pieces of advice about gaining relevant work experience based on accounts of personal experiences.

- ➲ *You can't send too many CVs!*
- ➲ *Everything with people is relevant – don't narrow your options.*
- ➲ *Be prepared to move around the country for jobs that you think are below your qualification level.*
- ➲ *There are so many hoops to jump through and so much to learn and it all seems to happen so slowly. If you don't enjoy this experience then consider carefully if this is for you.*
- ➲ *Contacts, Contacts, Contacts! Get to know the clinical psychologists working in your area.*
- ➲ *Persistence seems to be the key, along with networking – I was taken aback when I realised how much depends on who you know.*
- ➲ *Gaining voluntary or paid experience with various client groups had been valuable work in helping me to gain confidence in my belief that this is the right career path as well as helping me to feel more comfortable working with various different individuals with varying difficulties.*
- ➲ *Take out student loans whilst at university because even if you don't need them then you'll need them to help support yourself if you do voluntary work. Bar work just doesn't pay quite enough!!*
- ➲ *Each piece of experience I have gained has led me into the next, so I wouldn't discount anything.*
- ➲ *It's important to remember when working for charities like MIND (National Association for Mental Health) or Rethink, formally the NSF (National Schizophrenia Fellowship) that they help people with severe and enduring mental illness, which can be a very difficult area to work in. It is therefore essential to ensure that you have time each week to talk to a qualified member of*

staff about your contact with the people who use the service and make sure at the beginning that you know exactly what your role is, and what is expected of you.

⇨ Apply to places where you can work alongside assistant psychologists and learn about their role.

⇨ University tutors are always conducting their own research so ask them if they need an assistant psychologist.

⇨ Don't look upon the experience you gain simply in terms of how good it is going to look on an application form but treat it as an end in itself.

⇨ If you really want to be a clinical psychologist then all the effort will be par for the course for you and your enthusiasm will shine through when you apply for jobs. If you don't want to make the effort then you should look for another career.

⇨ Try to gain experience working with the kinds of client groups that you would like to work with as an assistant psychologist as this increases your chances of getting a post in that specific area.

⇨ Get a driver's licence because non-drivers can be excluded from many jobs.

PREVIOUS CAREERS

Whilst the majority of respondents decided to pursue a career in clinical psychology straight after their undergraduate degree, 31 per cent of the participants stated that they did have another career prior to becoming an assistant psychologist. Below are some examples of the kinds of careers participants came from and the reasons that they gave for making this change. As you will see there is quite a wide variety; you seem to be able to move to clinical psychology from all sorts of background experiences.

Professional ice-skater - 'I changed for a longer-term career'.

Education welfare officer - 'I wanted to be the person I referred the children to.'

Forensic psychologist - 'I moved for more money, and due to my current lack of career prospects and limited job role.'

Care worker for social services - 'I felt unchallenged and frustrated with my role and I had always wanted to do psychology.'

Nurse - 'Nursing is too task orientated and there is not enough scope for personal development.'

Administrator in a factory office - 'I changed to take up a more challenging career.'

Self-employed therapist in a complementary health centre - 'I decided to change because I felt isolated without colleague teamwork, and to broaden my knowledge base. I often felt ill-equipped to deal with clients since I worked on pragmatic, heuristic principles rather than from a strong theoretical base. Also, I wanted more direction and career path opportunities.'

Marketing executive - 'I changed because I hated it.'

Chef - 'I changed careers because I was not using my capabilities to their full potential.'

Exporter for the motor industry - 'There was a lack of long-term security.'

Researcher (dental) - 'I changed as I never intended to get into dental research, and always wanted to work within Clinical Psychology.'

Worker in housing and voluntary sector mental health projects - 'I decided to pursue Clinical Psychology due to its career structure and type of work it offered which I was interested in.'

Manager in a learning disability day service - 'I wasn't using my psychological skills, and the job wasn't challenging enough.'

Administrator - 'There was no job satisfaction and no challenge or variability to my work.'

Analyst/programmer - 'I wanted more personal contact, opportunities to help others and an academic challenge.'

Insurance - 'I realised I was soulless.'

Lawyer - 'I changed because there was not enough "people contact".'

3 | Applying for assistant psychologist Jobs

The competition for assistant psychologist jobs is very high; hence the effort that people often go to prior to getting a post. The number of applicants for a job varies tremendously but various rumours suggest that it is common for over one hundred psychology graduates to apply. This depends on both the job itself and where the job is advertised. National newspapers and the BPS Appointments Memorandum, for example, tend to have more applicants than local newspapers or internally advertised jobs. It is therefore very important to have some knowledge about what you are applying for and to perfect both application and interview techniques in order to stand a chance of getting a post.

WHERE TO LOOK FOR ASSISTANT PSYCHOLOGIST POSTS

Below is a list of all the sources that assistant psychologists suggested were worth using when looking for assistant psychologist posts.

- ➲ BPS Appointments Memorandum (sent out monthly with *The Psychologist* to members of the British Psychological Society) One of the most popular sources
- ➲ In England – the *Guardian* (Tuesdays, Wednesdays, and sometimes on Saturdays)
- ➲ In Scotland – the *Herald* and the *Scotsman*
- ➲ In Wales – the *Western Mail*
- ➲ In Ireland – the *Belfast Telegraph* and the *Irish Independent*
- ➲ Local newspapers (this is a good way of applying for jobs which are likely to have fewer applicants)
- ➲ Regional assistant psychologist groups (contact the DCP Affiliates Group for details)
- ➲ Internally advertised job lists (contact your local departments)
- ➲ University departments
- ➲ Internet (for example, www.psychjobs.co.uk or www.psychologyjobs.org.uk)
- ➲ Use your contacts or write to clinical psychology departments or personnel departments (addresses can be gained from your library under Health Service Information)

WHEN TO LOOK FOR ASSISTANT PSYCHOLOGIST POSTS

There was a variety of suggestions regarding the best time to look for assistant psychologist posts. The majority of posts tend to get advertised between May and October. This is the time in which people leave their jobs if they have got a place on a clinical psychology training course. However, assistant psychologist jobs are advertised throughout the whole year and it is still also worth being proactive in contacting departments or individuals.

ASSISTANT PSYCHOLOGIST POSTS STATISTICS

Amongst the participants who completed the questionnaire the lowest number of jobs applied to prior to gaining an assistant psychologist post was 0 and the highest was hundreds!! If you get a number of rejections it is important to remember that this is very common. Many people have similar experiences, and therefore do not get too disheartened by it. There appears to be no real average number of applications that you can expect to complete: 42 per cent applied for up to five jobs before getting their first assistant psychologist post, another 34 per cent applied for between five and fifty jobs, and roughly 10 per cent applied for over fifty jobs (with some into triple figures). Of the participants 84 per cent had been to up to four interviews prior to getting their first job, with the highest number of unsuccessful interviews one person had being fifteen.

These statistics illustrate the massive variability in experiences assistant psychologists had when applying for jobs. You cannot predict how long it will take but the most obvious predictive factor would probably be prior work experience. Berry (1997) describes a study of 150 applications for assistant psychologist posts in a special hospital, which provides an insight into the type of competition people face.

WHAT TO LOOK OUT FOR IN JOB DESCRIPTIONS

Below is a list of some of the most important things that you could look out for in a job description as highlighted in completed questionnaires:

- ➲ The amount and type of clinical work
- ➲ The amount and type of research work

- ➲ The amount and type of administrative work
- ➲ 'Supervision, supervision and supervision.' The level of supervision and who it is from (it should be from a qualified clinical psychologist)
- ➲ The person specification – make sure it matches your experience
- ➲ The amount of contact with other professionals you will be working with (for example, working alongside clinical psychologists and also multidisciplinary teams is important)
- ➲ Links with clinical psychology doctorate training courses
- ➲ Amount of peer support from other assistant psychologists and/or trainees in the area. If there are no other assistant psychologists or trainees there then you could join your local assistant psychologists group
- ➲ Training/teaching opportunities (both for being trained and being involved in carrying out training)
- ➲ Length of contract and if it is renewable
- ➲ Whether you need a car
- ➲ Adherence to BPS guidelines for employment of an assistant psychologist
- ➲ Whether you will be part of a team because working alone can be difficult
- ➲ Background details about the service
- ➲ Opportunities for professional development time
- ➲ How this post will help you to develop your curriculum vitae
- ➲ If the post interests you
- ➲ The variety of duties involved
- ➲ Academic qualifications required (for example, many posts will specify that the applicant must have an upper second class degree or above)
- ➲ Experience required (for example, some posts state that they would prefer somebody who has previously worked as an assistant psychologist or worked in some capacity with a certain client group)

- ⮑ Spine points available (wages). Remember that research assistant psychologists tend to be better paid than assistant psychologists
- ⮑ If the department has had assistant psychologists before and if they did what they did in the job, and what they went on to do

And beware . . .

- ⮑ the data entry clerk post dressed up as an assistant psychologist post
- ⮑ you're not just a dogsbody
- ⮑ working 'on shifts', often worded as 'implementing care plans'
- ⮑ posts that 'imply' direct care/personal care may be involved because some posts just use you as an additional care assistant psychologist
- ⮑ the post that is a thinly disguised administrative job

It can be difficult to get a real idea about the job from the description given as they can all look quite similar. It can therefore be a good idea to contact the relevant people in order to get a better idea about the specific details of the job. Alternatively a few people took a different slant when answering this question, for example, one of the participants stated: 'I don't think that the job description is at all important for your first assistant psychologist job. The important thing is to get the job with the assistant psychologist title then it isn't so difficult to move on to another job, which you think will suit you better.'

ADDITIONAL ADVICE FROM ASSISTANT PSYCHOLOGISTS

- ⮑ *Don't lie, but if you have transferable skills sell yourself and say so.*

- *Don't be afraid to ask for improvements if necessary.*
- *Don't forget to use the person specification to shape your answers on the application form.*
- *It's definitely better if you can drive and if you have a car.*
- *I think it is always nicer to work in departments where there are other assistant psychologists for support.*
- *Remember to keep a copy of your application form and the job description once you have sent off your application.*
- *If possible talk to the previous assistant psychologist. Assistant psychologist posts that come recommended are always good.*
- *Type your form if possible because this will not only make it look better but will allow more space for more details.*
- *Try to get your first post in a field you have experience in as this will probably be easier to do and you can then side step to other assistant psychologist posts.*
- *It is better not to use abbreviations in your application form.*
- *Do not overuse bold and italics.*
- *Don't flatter.*
- *Don't try to be funny, use colloquialisms or exclamation marks.*
- *I found ringing and meeting the supervisor prior to selection very helpful.*
- *You need to make sure that you're eligible for BPS graduate membership or better still are a graduate member.*
- *Make sure you phone for an application form as soon as possible as they can sometimes run out of forms because so many people are interested.*
- *If there is no specific job description with the application form then be careful because some assistant psychologist posts are created simply to prevent funds being*

> *withdrawn from a department who cannot fill a qualified*
> *clinical psychology post.*
> ⮑ *Get people to read your application forms and listen to*
> *what they say!*
> ⮑ *A calm, thoughtful impression is better than being overly*
> *excited and enthusiastic.*
> ⮑ *Even if the closing date for the application has passed*
> *you could still phone the personnel department to check*
> *if they would accept your application.*
> ⮑ *Think carefully about the language you use on your form*
> *and be sure to use politically correct terminology as this*
> *can say something about your views and can also be*
> *quite influential.*
> ⮑ *Get feedback.*
> ⮑ *Don't lose heart and keep trying!*

GUIDELINES FOR THE EMPLOYMENT OF AN ASSISTANT PSYCHOLOGIST

The British Psychological Society's Division of Clinical Psychology published guidelines for the employment of an assistant psychologist (Division of Clinical Psychology, 1998). It is worth bearing these guidelines in mind when applying for jobs and keep them in mind once employed as an assistant psychologist in order to ensure that the job is fulfilling them. If you have any problems it could be worth discussing this with your supervisor and using this document as back up.

The document provides guidance about the responsibilities and balance of work, particular issues relating to client work, the induction provided when starting work, supervision and study time amongst other things. Below are a few points incorporated into the document that were important to the assistant psychologists who completed the questionnaires.

> ⮕ A minimum of one hour's supervision from a qualified
> clinical psychologist should be provided every week.

- At least one session (half a day) should be allocated each week to study time.
- Peer support should be accessible.
- An assistant psychologist should not act as a substitute for qualified clinical psychologists or work alone with complex cases.
- An assistant psychologist should not carry out administrative work alone or carry out the duties of a care assistant psychologist.
- There should be formal induction procedures in place for the assistant psychologist when starting the job.

WHICH JOBS TO APPLY FOR

Some people stated that it is it is important only to apply for jobs in areas that interest you. Others said that it is good to get any assistant psychologist job to begin with and not be picky but keep the postman busy with all your application forms.

4 | Assistant psychologist job interviews

After getting so far it would be silly to throw it all away by not preparing for the interview. No two interviews are the same but there are some basic rules that can be applied to both preparing for an interview and the actual interview itself.

Assistant psychologists who completed the questionnaire were asked to reflect on their personal experiences of interviews and contribute any advice that that they considered useful with regards to the whole interview process. A lot of the information below is relevant to interviews in general, and some of it is specifically useful for interviews for assistant psychologist posts. For more information on interviews in general you could contact your local careers department who should have relevant literature.

PREPARING FOR AN INTERVIEW

Below are some tips from assistant psychologists that you may find useful when preparing for an interview.

- *Do read up on the relevant field but not in too much detail.*
- *Research the department and its specific speciality. If possible try to speak to other assistant psychologists to find out exactly what is required.*
- *If you haven't had an assistant psychologist's post before then think about how skills and experience you do have are transferable to this job.*
- *Read up on your dissertation because they almost always ask about it.*

- Think about the role of a psychologist and of an assistant psychologist in this service.
- Know exactly what is on your application form and be able to expand on it.
- Think about the client group and the kind of psychological problems they might have and possible input from clinical psychology.
- Read up on the latest governmental policy for the client group and general NHS initiatives.

- Be clear about why you want that job in particular as opposed to why you want to be an assistant psychologist/clinical psychologist in general.
- Think about what you have learnt from your undergraduate course and how it relates to the job (see Hayes, 1989).
- If you do not have experience of this client group that you could talk about but do have experience of other

groups then consider how any general approaches or issues could relate.

⤳ Think about possible questions that you might be asked and how you would approach them.

⤳ Be different! Try to think of some experience that you have which will make you stand out.

⤳ Look up any papers or books that the interviewers have published to get an idea of the type of work they carry out.

⤳ Practise using mock interviews and if possible try to get a video recording of a practice interview because this can reveal a lot that you may not be aware of.

⤳ Make sure that you understand the importance of supervision.

⤳ Have a description ready of a paper you've read recently.

⤳ Re-read the job advert for key phrases that may give a clue as to the skills sought by the interviewers and how they relate to you.

⤳ Prepare questions that you could ask the panel.

If you can, try to arrange an informal visit to the department prior to the interview.

THE INTERVIEW PROCESS

Below are some tips from assistant psychologists that you might find useful for the interview itself.

⤳ Relate everything back to you and your experiences. Anyone can memorise a textbook answer.

⤳ Try to relate theory to practice and vice versa so you can answer questions 'in theory' if you haven't had the experience and vice versa.

⤳ Relax. It's difficult but you are interviewing them too. At least they think you want the job and have the right sort of experience or they would not be interviewing you.

⤳ Be yourself.

- Dress smartly.
- Smile and if you don't know the answer be honest, don't make it up.
- Give yourself plenty of time to get there and arrive early so that you can talk to the staff before your interview.
- Be confident in your abilities and enthusiastic about the work. Convince yourself before the interview that you are the best person for the job and visualise yourself in the job.
- Don't try to know everything. I'm sure that interviewers are looking for someone who can adapt their experiences and skills rather than someone that thinks they 'know it all'! Most of all, they'll be looking for someone that they think they'll like and get on with!
- It can be useful to express that you are interested in applying for clinical training but be careful not to emphasise this too much as it may seem like the job is simply a means to an end, which they may not like.
- Just try and sell yourself as much as you can, even if you sound bigheaded!
- Acknowledge your limitations but don't dwell on them.
- If you are unsure about a question ask for it to be repeated or clarified, or for time to think instead of waffling.
- If there are any promises made to you at interview, for example, a place on an MSc course, then it is important to find out all the details of this and ask for it to be included in your contract.
- Do be critical of research that is discussed in interview if you can see things you would change about it instead of just complimenting it, but do not do this simply for the sake of it.
- If you don't get the job ask for feedback from the interviewer and make notes so that you don't make the same mistake next time.

➔ *It's not what you've done that the interviewers are interested in but what you've learnt from what you've done.*

➔ *If all else fails then imagine the interviewers naked. This should help you to relax.*

In describing their personal experiences of interviews for assistant psychologist posts, participants illustrated the extreme variability between interviews. There appears to be no set format because some interviews can be quite informal and chatty, whilst others can be very formal and involve presentations, group exercises or statistical tests amongst other things. It is therefore important to find out what the format for the interview will be so that you can prepare accordingly.

If you are not successful then try to remember that often employers are in a position where they have to choose between a number of good candidates. By getting to the interview stage you have done extremely well and are halfway there, so with some perseverance your luck could change. Next time you will have more of an advantage because you will be able to utilise what you have learnt from past interview experience.

5 | The role of an assistant psychologist

Responses from assistant psychologists regarding the type of work they carry out in their roles varied greatly. Some roles focused mostly on clinical work and some on research work, and others consisted of a mixture of both. There are also numerous additional tasks that people are required to carry out to varying degrees. Like a qualified clinical psychologist, an assistant psychologist can also find themselves juggling many tasks at once.

CLINICAL WORK

Assessment

A lot of assistant psychologist posts involve carrying out psychological assessments of clients and/or their carers or staff. This is done quantitatively and qualitatively through the use of questionnaires and/or semi-structured interviews. Below are a few specific examples from completed questionnaires of the kinds of assessments that assistant psychologists carry out.

- Depression and anxiety in newly diagnosed cancer patients
- Stress and burn out in health professionals
- Expressed emotion amongst carers of people with psychosis
- Risk with clients in a forensic setting
- Neuropsychological assessments of older adults with memory problems
- Neuropsychological assessments of people with brain injuries

Interventions

The amount of clinical intervention work and the level of the work that assistant psychologists carry out can vary greatly between posts. It is therefore crucial to take this into account when considering applying for or accepting an assistant psychologist post. Whilst it is important to gain experience of clinical interventions, it is also important that the work you carry out is of a suitable level. It would, for example, be inappropriate for an assistant psychologist to carry out work in place of a qualified clinical psychologist, though it would be appropriate for an assistant psychologist to work alongside a clinical psychologist with part of an intervention. This should all be negotiated with the assistant psychologist's supervisor with the previous experience of the individual taken into account. Whatever the intervention and degree of involvement, it is essential that all clinical work is closely and regularly supervised for the benefit of all parties involved.

Clinical work can be carried out with a variety of individuals or groups within a range of services. Below is a list of the kinds of clinical interventions that assistant psychologists can be involved in. This list is not exhaustive but contains examples from the questionnaire responses.

- ⮂ Anxiety management
- ⮂ Anger management
- ⮂ Pain management
- ⮂ Assertiveness training
- ⮂ Social skills training
- ⮂ Parenting skills training
- ⮂ Behaviour modification programmes
- ⮂ Behavioural interventions
- ⮂ Graded exposure
- ⮂ Systematic desensitisation
- ⮂ Relaxation therapy
- ⮂ Relapse prevention interventions
- ⮂ Basic protocol-driven interventions for mild to moderate mental health problems, such as agoraphobia, obsessive compulsive disorder, postnatal depression, post-traumatic stress disorder, social phobia, depression, and anxiety

RESEARCH WORK

Stages of research

There are a number of stages to carrying out research which are listed below. Assistant psychologists can get involved in some or all of these stages.

- ⮂ Literature searches and reviews
- ⮂ Designing research protocols
- ⮂ Designing questionnaires or semi-structured interviews

- Administration of questionnaires
- Semi-structured interviewing of participants
- Liaising with other professionals and participants for recruitment purposes
- Liaising with steering groups, policy makers, ethics committees etc.
- Carrying out interventions being evaluated
- Designing and maintaining databases
- Scoring questionnaires
- Data collection
- Data entry
- Data analysis (using various statistical packages)
- Writing reports, journal articles or conference posters
- Presenting findings (for example, at conferences or to your department)

Research projects

Below are some examples of research projects that people who completed the questionnaire have been involved in whilst working as assistant psychologists.

- The relationships between self-esteem, symptomatology and expressed emotion in recent-onset schizophrenia
- The psychological effects of asthma
- Personality change after traumatic brain injury
- The benefits of voice therapy
- Early detection and intervention in psychosis
- The effect of operations under general anaesthesia on the cognitive functioning of older adults
- Physical health needs of people with learning disabilities
- Quality of life in cataract patients
- Developing a questionnaire measure on fitness to go on trial with people with a mental illness who have been charged with a crime

> ⊃ Evaluation of dementia assessments for people with learning disabilities

Some assistant psychologists carry out research in their job as part of a further qualification (such as a master's degree or a doctorate). Gaining such a qualification allows you to further develop your research skills and also looks good on your curriculum vitae.

Audit

It is also quite common for assistant psychologist posts to involve audit work, for example, evaluating the services provided and the needs of service users or professionals working within a service. Audit is increasingly popular within psychology departments and plays a key role in the latest government initiatives for the NHS as a whole. It requires carrying out similar processes to research. Below are some examples of audit work that assistant psychologists who completed the questionnaire have carried out.

> ⊃ What young people make of the experience of attending adolescent psychiatry
> ⊃ Multi-disciplinary assessments and outreach services
> ⊃ The need for a psychology service
> ⊃ The pathways into inpatient service and treatment across different ethnic groups
> ⊃ The use of administration and clerical services of a psychology department
> ⊃ Client and carer satisfaction of a day-care service for early-onset dementia

OTHER TASKS

In addition to clinical and research work, assistant psychologists carry out a range of other tasks. Below is a list of the kinds of tasks that assistant psychologists carry out. People will not be expected to carry out all of the tasks on the list but most assistant psychologists seem to carry out at least a few of them.

- Shadowing clinical psychologists
- Attending various meetings (for example, departmental or team meetings)
- Attending ward rounds and feeding back information about clients
- Attending care programme approach reviews
- Writing reports (for example, of a neuropsychological assessment)
- Liaising with clients and/or families/carers
- Liaising with members of multidisciplinary teams
- Administration (for example, photocopying, correspondence and filing)
- Literature searches
- Creating and maintaining resources for the department (for example, professional literature)
- Creating literature for clients, carers or other professionals regarding services, diagnosis etc.
- Developing and maintaining databases (for example, client information databases)
- Developing training packs
- Teaching and training of professionals in related fields (for example, community psychiatric nurses, psychiatric ward staff)
- Organising workshops, talks or conferences

THE IMPORTANCE OF EXPERIENCE GAINED AS AN ASSISTANT PSYCHOLOGIST

There were three main points made in answer to the question, 'How important is the above experience for an assistant psychologist and why?' Firstly, it was suggested that all the above experience, and simply working within an environment alongside clinical psychologists, provides the opportunity to find out if this is really the profession for you. One participant explained that 'it really gives you a feel for exactly what the clinical psychologists in your department actually do on a day-to-day basis - warts and all!'

Secondly, the general view was that both clinical and research experience is very important, both because clinical psychologists carry out such work, and also to help you 'develop skills necessary to prepare for clinical training'. A mixture of both clinical and research work also allows you to gain a deeper understanding of the relationship between theory and practice which will also help with an application for the clinical psychology training courses.

Thirdly, in addition to the research and clinical experience, it was noted that some of the other tasks are also very beneficial. The role of a clinical psychologist does not stop at research and clinical work. Therefore the opportunity to be involved in liaising with other professionals from multi-disciplinary teams, service evaluation and development, and teaching and training, for example, also provides insight into the varied role of a clinical psychologist within the changing culture of the NHS. In addition this variety of roles allows you to develop a number of useful skills that you will be able to use again in training and once qualified.

It must also be noted, however, as many of the completed questionnaires did, that some of the tasks can be mundane and seemingly of little benefit in the long term. For example, many assistant psychologists will have horror stories to tell about their experiences of fighting with a photocopier. Unfortunately this is simply the nature of the work, and again it varies from job to job.

In summary, it would seem that research and clinical work are the most important kinds of experience but that many of the other tasks mentioned are also very useful too. It was widely advised that people should look for a variety of work opportunities. If a post appears only to offer experience in one of the areas it is worth enquiring about other areas as well. The more rounded your experience, the more you learn about the diverse roles of a clinical psychologist, and once armed with these skills the more confident you will feel and come across when applying for the clinical psychology training courses.

In order to gain the most from your job it can therefore be beneficial to use your initiative to increase the quality of experience you get. Harvey and Tait (1999) describe their experience of organising a training programme for assistant psychologists in their trust that was taught by various members of qualified staff who agreed to help. Being involved in such a project would both increase your opportunities for training on the job and also look impressive to future employees or courses.

DIFFERENT CLIENT GROUPS

There are many different clinical specialities that you can work in as an assistant psychologist. Below is a list placed in order according to the percentage of participating assistant psychologists who were working in that speciality at the time of completing the questionnaire. Due to the continually changing state of assistant psychologist posts in all areas it is difficult to estimate the proportion of assistant psychologists who work in various specialities nationally. It is worth bearing in mind therefore that these percentages are not necessarily representative of assistant psychologists nationally but simply of those who completed the questionnaires. Also, this is not an exhaustive list of all the areas that use clinical psychology services, there are many more. However it does give a good idea of the kinds of areas worked in and that assistant psychologist posts can be based within both general clinical areas, such as adult mental health, and also specific clinical problems, such as working with people with eating disorders or autism.

Often people can find that some of these specialities overlap, for example, working with adults with learning disabilities and mental health problems. Similarly, some posts involve working within more than one speciality, for example, a split post between adult mental health and older adult mental health.

- ➲ Learning disabilities – 25%
- ➲ Adult mental health – 20%

- Children and adolescents with mental health problems (and their families) – 18%
- Older adults with mental health problems – 12%
- Neuropsychology (including problem areas such as acquired brain injury, strokes, Parkinson's disease, dementia and meningitis) – 12 per cent
- Forensic mental health – 12%
- Challenging behaviours – 5%
- Psychosis – 4%
- Addiction services – 3%
- Eating disorders – 2%
- Chronic pain– 2%
- Adults with voice disorders – 1%
- Cancer patients suffering from depression and anxiety – 1%
- Autism – 1%
- Borderline personality disorder – 1%

REASONS FOR WORKING WITH DIFFERENT CLIENT GROUPS

There appeared to be a number of reasons that led participants to be working within a specific area of clinical psychology. These reasons tended to fall into the four main categories specified below.

- They had a personal interest in the speciality due to prior work experience with this client group or teaching on their undergraduate courses and thought that this would be beneficial in their work.
- They had previously worked in another speciality and wanted to move in order to vary their experience. This usually applied to people who had been in more than one assistant psychologist post.
- They had not chosen the speciality but taken the job for the general experience of being an assistant

psychologist. As one person stated: 'Can we be choosey at this stage?' This was a very common response.

⮑ The job provided a range of experience (for example, both research and clinical) and it was therefore the variability of the work that appealed more than the speciality itself.

THE PROS AND CONS OF WORKING WITH DIFFERENT CLIENT GROUPS

The participants were asked what they thought were the good and bad points of working within their speciality. Below are just a few of the responses given. A key point to note, however, is that there are a lot of other variables to consider which contribute to the kind of experience that each job gives you. Examples of such factors include: the department facilities, supervision, other professionals, degree of responsibility, etc. These factors can also influence people's individual perceptions of working with certain client groups.

Adult mental health

- Working as an assistant psychologist in adult mental health can be quite straightforward and it is a good speciality for your first post. You can then apply these skills when working within other specialities.
- There are set protocols to follow for many of the issues which may arise and you can therefore feel quite well guided.
- This is one of the better-funded specialities in terms of clinical practice and research.
- A high proportion of clients do not attend appointments due to long waiting lists or work, amongst other things.
- Clinical psychology is not as involved in working with families and/or carers as they are in some other specialities.
  This area can feel more like a treadmill approach.

Children/adolescents

- It is good to be part of the process that helps them to make positive changes at an early age, which then influence the rest of their lives.
- You often get the opportunity to work with parents and teachers as well, which widens your experience further but can be frustrating too if they think you should be working solely with the child.
- Working with this client group requires you to be very creative and use your imagination.
- It can involve very little contact with the children and more work with parents.
- It is sometimes hard working with young people with mental health problems because it's easy to become too involved.
- It can be upsetting because there is a high incidence of abuse.

Older adults

- ◌ It can involve a lot of work with families and/or carers which makes your work more varied.
- ◌ The people are often so grateful and friendly and let you know that what you are doing makes a difference.
- ◌ It can be very interesting working with people who have such a wealth of life experience.
- ◌ This group is sometimes not very psychologically minded so you have to spend time building rapport and being creative with interventions.
- ◌ You can come face-to-face with severe physical illness, people losing their independence, and death quite a lot, which can be distressing.
- ◌ It is not as high profile as some other areas and so there can be problems with a lack of necessary resources.

Learning disabilities

- ◌ Working in learning disabilities you can encounter a mixture of problems alongside the learning disability, which is challenging.
- ◌ Requires working closely in multidisciplinary teams.
- ◌ Clients can make small changes, which mean a lot.
- ◌ People wrongly assume that all behaviour is caused by the learning disability, which can be frustrating.
- ◌ These clients are undervalued by society and you often have to fight for people's rights when they should be automatic.
- ◌ It can be hard to overcome communication barriers so you need to be very creative.

ADDITIONAL ADVICE FROM ASSISTANT PSYCHOLOGISTS

Below is a list of some key points from assistant psychologists in various specialities to bear in mind before you begin to work with any new client group.

- *Read up about key problems facing the client group, the assessment procedures and interventions that are commonly used, as well as the latest research trends and professional issues that are important when working with this group.*
- *Make sure you have good supervision.*
- *Listen to clients' and carers' views.*
- *Speak to people who work with the client group or know anything about it.*
- *Listen a lot and don't be shy to ask questions as you won't be expected to know everything.*
- *Make the most of any support systems that are available when you begin to work with a new client group because it can be very daunting.*
- *Find out about department policies for working with clients, for example, regarding suicide risk.*
- *Think about the concerns that the client may have about their contact with psychology services, as well as any concerns that you have.*
- *Try to get in touch with an assistant psychologist who works with this client group to find out about the kind of work that an assistant psychologist is expected to do.*
- *If you are considering working with a certain client group you could do some voluntary work or visit an appropriate service to gain an insight into what it would be like.*
- *Make the most of any opportunities to work with other related professionals and see what work they carry out with the client group.*
- *Make the most of any training opportunities.*

> ⮑ *Take it slowly, and try to observe qualified clinicians when you first start.*
>
> ⮑ *Begin with an open mind.*

PROFESSIONAL DEVELOPMENT

One of the points that has been made repeatedly is that the experience gained as an assistant psychologist allows you to begin your training in the profession, which should continue to play a significant role throughout your career. Many qualified staff are allocated time for professional development, and many assistant psychologist posts also provide this opportunity. There is currently a general move-ment to ensure that this is provided throughout the whole profession and that it is used appropriately. It is worthwhile ensuring that you will have such an opportunity in a post and it is worth making the most of such time. Guidelines for the employment of an assistant psychologist published by the DCP state that professional development should be part of the job.

Professional development/study time can be used for work that is not directly related to your job but is relevant to the profession. For example, you could use it for doing a piece of research, working with clients in a different speciality, doing voluntary work for another service, general reading, attending workshops or conferences and so on. This should be agreed with your supervisor. When deciding what to do with this time it is worth taking into account what experience you already have and what you need to build on. This is a great chance for widening the variety of your experience, as discussed earlier. For example, if you are only doing research in your role, it could be useful to enquire about possibilities for doing some clinical work.

SUPERVISION

Supervision is an essential element to the work carried by qualified clinical psychologists, trainee clinical psychologists and assistant psychologists. Supervision is extremely important when working as an assistant psychologist and there are guidelines for supervision set out in the DCP Guidelines for the employment of assistant psychologists. Birnie (1997) and Webb and Dodd (2001) both present useful guidelines for the supervision of assistant psychologists that can be helpful for both assistant psychologists and supervisors to follow. Fleming and Steen's book about supervision in clinical psychology (forthcoming 2003) also has relevance for anyone working in this field.

It is relevant to discuss supervision at this stage because the type and amount of supervision provided contributes greatly to the quality of the post. Supervision is not an option but essential to the work of an assistant psychologist. It should be provided by a qualified clinical psychologist and take place for at least one hour each week. Assistant psychologists should take an active role in their supervision in order to optimise the benefits that can be gained from it.

Supervision provides an opportunity for the assistant psychologist to seek guidance regarding any problems they are having with clients, research work or any other of their tasks. It also serves to ensure that the assistant psychologist is gaining relevant experience and skills to enhance their application for clinical psychology training courses. Similarly, it allows supervisors to monitor the work that is carried out by the assistant psychologist and ensure that it is of a good standard and being done appropriately. Supervision is therefore an essential element of an assistant psychologist job not only for the benefit of the assistant psychologist but also for the employer and the clients involved too.

If you find yourself in a position where you are not receiving appropriate supervision then it is important to do something about this. You could approach your supervisor if you feel able to do so, and use the DCP guidelines for the employment of an assistant psychologist for support, or you could seek out other ways of gaining support from your peers through local assistant psychologist groups. It is also worth remembering that you are not alone since there is wide variation in the quality of supervision received by assistant psychologists across the country. This is noted by Gallagher and Brosnan (2001) who carried out a study to evaluate the supervision experiences of assistant psychologists, which were found on the whole to be positive but 'patchy'. There is certainly no good excuse for it but should help you to feel less isolated in your situation.

THE PROS AND CONS OF BEING AN ASSISTANT PSYCHOLOGIST

Although there was not a section within the questionnaire regarding the pros and cons of being an assistant psychologist, there were a number of requests for this to be included in the write up. Throughout the questionnaire many people stated things that they enjoyed and things that they did not like about being assistant psychologists. These varied greatly which is reflective of the extreme variability in the quality of assistant psychologist posts. When considering applying for assistant psychologist posts it could be worth taking into consideration some of the key themes that emerged from the questionnaires regarding this topic which are listed below.

Pros

- ⮕ Working alongside clinical psychologists and gaining insight into the work that they carry out
- ⮕ Carrying out a variety of roles within one job
- ⮕ Working independently
- ⮕ Expanding on research skills gained from degrees
- ⮕ Observing and carrying out supervised clinical work
- ⮕ Working with other health care professionals
- ⮕ Working with a variety of client groups and in a wide range of health care settings
- ⮕ Carrying out rewarding work that can make a difference to people's lives
- ⮕ Using the theory learnt in your degree in practice
- ⮕ Receiving continuous training
- ⮕ Getting involved in teaching and training

- ➲ Gaining an understanding of the role of clinical psychology within the NHS
- ➲ Carrying out challenging work
- ➲ Entering a lifelong career path

Cons

- ➲ Feelings of isolation (especially in smaller departments)
- ➲ Lack of quality and quantity of supervision
- ➲ Carrying out tasks one is inadequately trained to do
- ➲ Lack of definition in role
- ➲ Exploitation and lack of respect because you are seen as being on the bottom rung of the ladder
- ➲ Poor induction
- ➲ Poor pay
- ➲ Lack of security due to short-term contracts
- ➲ Carrying out tasks that are basic and tedious (e.g. fighting with a photocopier)

the role of an assistant psychologist

Tattershall et al. (1997) noted some of these issues in an article describing the rewards and drawbacks of being an assistant psychologist. These issues were also highlighted by Rezin and Tucker (1998) who describe the outcome of a survey completed by assistant psychologists about their roles. Their findings unfortunately highlight that the guidelines set by the DCP for the employment of assistant psychologists are not always followed and identify two types of 'problem assistant psychologist posts'. One is the 'under used' post where 'the assistant psychologist has a lack of defined role, a lack of training and has little confidence in his/her skills. There are feelings of isolation and confidence is low'. The other is the 'too much' post where 'the assistant psychologist has not enough supervision for inappropriate clients and may have experienced bad or frightening situations with clients. Understandably they have a lack of confidence in patient outcomes and their own skills. They feel undervalued compared to trainees, but far too much is expected of them'. They suggest that their survey provides 'clear and uncomfortable evidence that assistant psychologists are working in abusive and unsafe situations' (Rezin and Tucker, 1998).

Their findings are similar to those of Harper and Newton (1988) a decade earlier, which suggest that this situation is not about to change in a hurry. However, assistant psychologists do seem to be raising these issues more and more through local groups and hopefully this will eventually result in positive changes. Black and Eccles (2000) put forward some suggestions for implementing the DCP guidelines from policy into practice. Hopefully articles will follow highlighting the implementation and evaluation of such suggestions.

6 | Applying for clinical psychology training

DEALING WITH THE PROCESS

Some people may decide that applying for clinical psychology training is not for them. However, all of the assistant psychologists who completed the questionnaire had applied or intended to apply. The questionnaire asked people how many times they had applied to clinical psychology training courses. 30 per cent had never applied, 36 per cent had applied once at the time of completing the questionnaire, 17 per cent had applied twice, 14 per cent had applied three times and 3 per cent had applied four times. There is a great deal of variability in the number of times people apply to the courses before gaining a place (or changing career paths). There are a number of factors that contribute to this variability, for example, the amount of experience that people have when they begin to apply.

When completing the questionnaire some people had already found out if they had been successful in securing a place on a course and others had not. Amongst those who had heard and been successful, some had applied up to four times and for others it had been their first application. There are a lot of rumours that accompany each stage of the application process, which you hear especially if you work alongside other assistant psychologists. It is a good idea to listen to them but not to take them too seriously. On a more useful note, there were some common themes that emerged in the personal descriptions and advice that people gave in relation to application and interview processes. These reflections came both from people who had been successful in securing a place on a course and those who had not. These are outlined below.

THE APPLICATION PROCESS

To apply for clinical psychology training courses you must contact the clearing house (see Appendix 4). There are a few courses that operate separately but the clearing house can provide details of these. You may want to refer back to Chapter 3 on applying for assistant psychologist posts because much of the advice is also relevant at this stage. In addition, and more specifically, below are some key points provided by assistant psychologists regarding application for clinical psychology training courses. This advice is based on their personal experiences.

Starting the form

⇨ *If you know any trainees, ask if you can look at their successful application forms to get an idea of what the courses are looking for. However, it is easy to get obsessed with what other applicants have written, rather than what you yourself have to offer. Remember this when looking at other forms.*

⇨ *Start filling in your form early as it is very time consuming.*

⇨ *Be warned that you can feel you have no control over the proceedings and you've got more chance of getting six numbers on the lottery.*

⇨ *Get a good draft then leave it alone completely for two weeks before coming back to it, re-reading it and amending it.*

⇨ *It can be difficult fitting your answers into the format but at least everybody is in the same boat.*

⇨ *Check very carefully that your degree course (particularly if it's a dual course) gives you graduate basis for registration with the BPS.*

⇨ *Try to get the buzzwords in.*

⇨ *Make yourself familiar with the points system they use to evaluate the form and play to your strengths.*

- Talking to other assistant psychologists/trainees is useful. Although it can seem to increase your stress levels, sharing ideas tends to pay off.
- Try to make sure that your referee gives you a good reference because references are very important to your scores. Make sure that you give your referees all of the information about you they need and ask for honest opinions on what they might say. If they are not willing to give you a very good reference then ask somebody else.
- Publications are not essential but always look good so mention any that you have under your belt.
- Do not exceed the space provided.
- Do not change the format.
- Try to link what you have done in relation to wider policies/legislation/frameworks, etc.
- Different training courses have different orientations and it's worth trying to find out about these and what would suit you.
- If you know of other people trying to get in try not to get caught up in the hysteria of it.
- Don't spend time focusing on what experience you haven't got but think about what you have done and its relevance to clinical psychology.
- When completing the last section of the form about past work experience it is important to talk about what you have learnt, not simply what you have done, and how this will help you as a trainee.
- Make it personal as the person reading it will read lots of others, and putting something in that is a bit different will help to get you noticed.

Checking the form

- Get a selection of different people to read your form. It is a particularly good idea to get clinical psychologists

> to read it, especially one who has some idea of how applications are rated.
>
> ⇒ Don't get too many people to look at your form because you may receive conflicting views.
>
> ⇒ I'd really recommend asking clinical psychologists that don't know you to read your form. Someone who knows you well will interpret your responses with this in mind. An objective appraisal is valuable.
>
> ⇒ Don't take the advice you are given too seriously because it is often contradictory.
>
> ⇒ Trainees and newly-qualified clinical psychologists probably give the most useful comments on forms than those who may be out of touch with the process.

When to apply

There were complete contradictions in the overall advice regarding a suitable time to apply. Some people suggested that applying even if you think your chances are very slim is a good idea. They suggest that there is nothing to be lost by doing so and that it makes the process easier the next time around because you have had the practice. On the other hand, some people stated that it only generates unnecessary stress and disappointment if you apply without a lot of experience.

THE INTERVIEW PROCESS

Chapter 4 has already covered some important points to consider when preparing for and going to interviews for assistant psychologist posts. Many of these points are also relevant to the clinical psychology training course interviews. In addition, below are some more suggestions made by assistant psychologists which relate directly to clinical psychology training course interviews. These are based on personal experiences and are worth considering too.

- Get familiar with NHS issues and recent white papers, etc.
- Organise a mock interview. It is probably better if possible to do this with people who do not know you very well.
- Prepare throughout the year by keeping up to date with literature, NHS changes, etc.
- Be prepared for questions which require some degree of self-disclosure (e.g. a traumatic event) and decide in advance the level of disclosure you feel comfortable with.
- Be prepared for the whole process to be extremely stressful. Lots of support from family/friends/colleagues is therefore helpful.
  Familiarise yourself with the orientation of the course (for example, cognitive behavioural or eclectic) and bear this in mind when you go for the interview.
- Try to find out prior to the interview how they format it so that you are prepared and practised in the approach.
- Revise with other assistant psychologists.
- Assistant psychologist groups are good for support and most clinical psychologists accept that their assistant psychologists all go a little crazy around Easter time!
- Remember that interviewers take your nerves into account.
- Be prepared to reflect on yourself as a person and how you would cope as a trainee.
- Try to get hold of questions from previous interviews and practise going through them with whoever will help.
- Be prepared to talk about some research you have been involved in and if you have not done any since your undergraduate course then refer back to this.
- Focus on your own experience with clients and colleagues and make sure that you can critically evaluate your experience, linking theory to practice.
- Talk to people who are already on the course about their experience at interview and on the course.

- Don't over-prepare because you will only use a very small percentage of it and it could serve to simply stress you out.
- Remember that 'practice makes perfect'!
- Seek out the reassurance of your peer group and eat more chocolate between March and June.

GETTING REJECTIONS

Getting rejections either from your application form or after interview can be very distressing. Below are a few pieces of advice from assistant psychologists who have been through this experience.

- It helps to have some positive thoughts to focus on, for example, think of how your next assistant psychologist's post could improve your experience and confidence, or think back to when you graduated and how much you have already achieved.
- Have alternative career interests. These don't have to be completely different.
- Plan a holiday for after all the interviews as something to look forward to.
- Remember that most people's working life is up to around the age of sixty-five. Even if you don't get on a course for a few years you'll probably have plenty of your professional lifetime left!
- Don't be discouraged or take things personally and remember that the selection process is not perfect.
- Persevere
- Try to get feedback from as many people as possible from the courses you apply to, though this can be very hard to achieve.
- If you are not successful it is important to listen to feedback and suggestions, but remember that the opinion is from one course only. Different courses want different

things. If you are unsure about the feedback it can be helpful to talk it over with your supervisor or someone who knows you well at work.

⇨ Make the most of your support systems because you will need them.

⇨ Focus on how you can improve for the following year by identifying weaknesses and ways to change them.

⇨ Keep copies of your form to look over during the following year.

⇨ Speak to other people who have been, or are, in the same position and understand what it feels like.

⇨ Although it's probably the last thing on your mind it is worth writing down your thoughts and feelings as soon as you can after the interview for future reference. It's surprising what you forget.

⇨ This is very difficult, but try not to think of getting on a course as the be-all-and-end-all.

ADVICE FROM COURSE DIRECTORS

Course directors across the country were sent a brief questionnaire asking for their views about people gaining experience as an assistant psychologist prior to applying to courses and about what they look for in applicants. Below is a list of some of the advice provided on completed questionnaires.

Advice on what courses may look for in an applicant

⇨ Someone who demonstrates a mature attitude and approach to their application. They may have the academic requirements and relevant experience but to be able to consolidate the two in an appropriate manner requires a flexible and assertive approach, recognition of their experience and knowledge but also of the gaps in these areas too.

- *An ethically-aware, thoughtful, enthusiastic individual who is able to link psychological knowledge to clinical problems/presentations. They must demonstrate an ability to use academic knowledge and know the value and limitations of research. Also a strong sense of self.*
- *Embryonic scientist-practitioners, essentially a scholarly attitude to knowledge, appropriate professional attributes and personal/interpersonal qualities.*
- *Good social skills, intelligent, hard working, commited to the NHS, good personal organisation and relevant experience.*
- *The sort of experience that successful applicants typically have are as an assistant psychologist within an NHS Trust, or as a psychology research assistant. Some applicants also have previous experience within a related discipline such as psychiatric nursing and social work or other clinically relevant areas. If applicants have a background in research, it is preferable if that research involves human subjects and is of clinical relevance. There should also be sufficient previous relevant experience to have enabled the candidate to gain some useful skills and knowledge, i.e. the experience should have been more than a few hours a week for a few months.*

Advice on the potential pros and cons of working as an assistant psychologist prior to training

- *It represents a 'pre-training induction' to NHS/psychology services and a general socialisation to the profession.*
- *The timing is important here. Too short a time as an assistant psychologist can leave the applicant unready and naïve, too long a time can make them over-ripened. Laying the experience-gaining years needs to be just that, laying the foundations and being exposed to the*

> issues. Too long a time leads to rigid ways of being and narrow views.

General advice for people wishing to pursue a career in clinical psychology

- ⊝ *Gain relevant experience as both an assistant psychologist and in research. Also look at other ways of gaining experience such as working as a nursing assistant psychologist.*
- ⊝ *Understand the role of a clinical psychologist and think why it appeals to you rather than seeking the 'right answer'. Integrate and reflect on your experience to help you develop a mature approach.*
- ⊝ *Explore what you don't know rather than focus on what you do know. Recognise limits and gaps and plan proactively to fill them in a considered way, recognising the problems and advantages along the way.*
- ⊝ *Develop an awareness of the range of roles clinical psychologists can take on.*
- ⊝ *Think again after three or four attempts.*
- ⊝ *Become aware of your emotional robustness and of your personal support.*
- ⊝ *Be persistent if this is what you really want.*
- ⊝ *Publish something; show evidence of tenacity. Work hard and try to have some tangible product of that work.*
- ⊝ *It is a great thing to do with your life but you will always find times when you have to struggle.*
- ⊝ *It is getting easier to get on courses – the number of places is increasing and the number of applicants falling, so keep trying.*

PLANNED EXPANSION OF TRAINING COURSES

At the time of writing there is planned expansion in training places in England of between 40 and 70 per cent over the next three years as stated in the NHS National Plan. There has also been a national drop in applications for courses. Statistically this therefore reduces the degree of competition for training places, which is very encouraging for anyone interested in pursuing a career in this profession.

7 | Applying for clinical psychology training

THE CLEARING HOUSE RESEARCH
PROJECT

Chris Hatton, Anna Phillips and Ian Gray

Lancaster University Doctorate in Clinical Psychology

INTRODUCTION

For many people, applying for clinical psychology training is a fraught process. Applicants are often convinced that clinical psychology training is incredibly competitive, and that the selection procedures used by training courses are unfair or effectively a lottery. Indeed, concerns from a number of sources have periodically been expressed about the fairness and validity of selection procedures to clinical psychology training, particularly in terms of equal opportunities issues.

This chapter aims to discuss the reality of applying to clinical psychology training courses, using available research evidence. In particular, this chapter will report initial findings from an ongoing research project, funded by the clearing house, which tracked the application process for all 1,538 applicants to clinical psychology training in the year 2000. Findings from this project and other sources will begin to answer some important questions for potential applicants, such as:

- ➲ What are my chances of success?
- ➲ Who applies to clinical psychology training?
- ➲ What selection procedures do training courses use?
- ➲ What factors are associated with shortlisting and
- ➲ selection to clinical psychology training?

WHAT ARE MY CHANCES OF SUCCESS?

One of the most durable beliefs of applicants to clinical psychology training is that training places are very competitive. In fact, throughout the 1990s the odds of gaining a training place have rapidly improved. In 1995, there were 1,398 applicants for 263 training places, with a 19 per cent chance of success. By 2001, there were 1,486 applicants for 454 training places, with a 31 per cent chance of success. Furthermore (as noted in the previous chapter), the current climate suggests further increases in the number of training places, with little evidence of a similar rise in the number of applicants. Of course, the number of applicants might increase in the future if training places begin to be seen as less competitive than they were.

WHO APPLIES?

The clearing house project coded the application forms of all applicants to clinical psychology training in the year 2000. In addition, data concerning additional information were obtained from questionnaires received from 396 applicants. Findings from this cohort are similar to those found in previous research concerning the demographic characteristics of applicants to clinical psychology training.

- 80% – female[a]
- 70% – under 30, 21% – 30–39[b]
- 90% – White[b]
- 95% – heterosexual[b]
- 11% long-standing illness or disability[b]
- 80% – social classes I and II, 3% social classes III and IV[b] (using parental occupation as an indicator of social class)
- 61% – single, 36% married or living as married[b]
- 17% – at least one dependant[b]
- 86% – access to independent transport[b]

Note: a = application form; b = questionnaire

This confirms the widely-held view that applicants to clinical psychology training are largely young, white, middle-class women without significant caring responsibilities.

Given the demographic characteristics of applicants, the typical educational experiences of applicants are unsurprising.

- ⮑ 94% had gained 'A' levels or Scottish Highers at school sixth forms or sixth-form colleges (or a foreign equivalent), with only 5% of applicants going through access courses
- ⮑ Those with 'A' levels had an average of three at Grade B; those with Scottish Highers had an average of five, also at Grade B
- ⮑ 95% had or were engaged in a single or joint honours degree in psychology
- ⮑ 7% were current undergraduates
- ⮑ Of those who had completed their degree: 13% 1st, 76% 2:1, 11% 2:2 and 1% 3rd
- ⮑ 86% had the British Psychological Society Graduate Basis for Registration
- ⮑ 5% were currently full-time postgraduate students; 34% had obtained or were enrolled for a masters qualification; 6% had obtained or were enrolled for a PhD
- ⮑ A small proportion had additional professional qualifications: 3% teaching, 6% nursing and 1% social work

Applicants had varied vocational experience, and had been in full-time employment for a median two years, almost all of which had been in NHS or related settings.

The most common form of employment for applicants was as an assistant psychologist, with 58 per cent of applicants having been employed in this capacity. Of all applicants 32 per cent had been in one post, 17 per cent in two posts and 9 per cent in three or more posts; 23 per cent of all applicants had been an assistant psychologist for less than a year, 24 per cent between one and two years, and 11 per cent for more than two years.

The other common form of employment was an academic post, usually a research assistant psychologist, with 31 per cent of applicants having been employed in this capacity. Of all applicants 22 per cent had been in one post, and 9 per cent in two or more posts; 15 per cent of all applicants had been in post for less than a year, 9 per cent between one and two years, and 7 per cent for more than two years. In terms of publications, 8 per cent of applicants were an author on one publication, and 9 per cent on two or more publications.

In terms of specialism, 90 per cent of applicants had worked in at least one major speciality; 36 per cent in one main speciality, 35 per cent in two specialities and 19 per cent in 3 or more specialities.

References for applicants were generally very positive. Almost all academic referees rated that applicants would get on well with clients (94 per cent), get on well with colleagues (95 per cent), be energetic and efficient (95 per cent) and be capable of independent work (98 per cent). The average rating of applicants (on a 1-5 scale) was 4. Experience-related referees were similarly positive, with almost all of them saying they would employ the applicant again (92 per cent).

WHAT SELECTION PROCEDURES DO COURSES USE?

As part of the clearing house project a national survey of all twenty-four clearing house training courses was conducted, asking them about the shortlisting and selection procedures they used for the 2000 intake of applicants.

Shortlisting

For shortlisting, courses used an average of three raters, of whom half were course staff. Almost all courses (96 per cent) used quantitative rating schemes to shortlist, and 87 per cent of courses gave shortlisters training and/or guidance on how to shortlist. Despite concerns expressed in previous research about low inter-rater reliability between shortlisters, only 64 per cent of courses calculated inter-rater reliability, although when reported inter-rater reliability was high. One problem for shortlisters is the relatively open response format of much of the application form, as evidence from graduate recruitment suggests that open-response formats in application forms are more likely to result in applicants making up answers to please the recruiter.

The majority of courses (88 per cent) also used reference forms during shortlisting, even though general organisational research has questioned the validity and reliability of open-response referee reports.

Selection

All courses used an interview as part of the selection procedure. Courses used an average of twelve interviewers, of which just under half (46 per cent) were course staff. Other interviewers varied widely across courses, including placement supervisors, local clinical psychologists, academics, health psychologists, human resources staff and trainees. Half the courses used the same interview panel throughout interviewing, and of those who did not, 88 per cent used standardised questions across the different panels. Again, only 32 per cent calculated inter-rater reliability between interviewers, although when reported inter-rater reliability was generally satisfactory.

The format of interviews was semi-structured for most courses (79 per cent), with only 17 per cent of courses using highly structured interviews and one course using an unstructured interview. These procedures are similar to those reported for courses almost ten years ago. However, organisational research suggests that the validity of semi-structured job interviews is questionable, as they are open to impression management by the candidate. In addition, interviewers are disproportionately likely to select candidates whom they personally like or perceive as similar to themselves.

Interviews for clinical psychology training varied widely in the types of questions asked and the rationale for their selection. The most common types of questions concerned core competencies (70 per cent of courses) and job-related questions (70 per cent). However, questions were most commonly selected according to the specific interests of courses

(70 per cent of courses) rather than the core competencies required (33 per cent) or a systematic job analysis (one course). Most courses (71 per cent) also used references during interviewing.

In addition to interviews, many courses used additional selection procedures: 25 per cent of courses used some type of oral presentation; 17 per cent of courses asked candidates to complete a written exercise/essay; two courses used an assessment centre style exercise; two courses held an informal social gathering; two courses used some type of performance test; one course asked candidates to do a case analysis; one course held a group discussion; one course asked candidates to do a role play and one course used a self-assessment examination/checklist.

Courses also reported great diversity in the characteristics of applicants they were attempting to select, including: clinical skills; academic skills; research skills; personal qualities; interpersonal abilities; problem-solving ability; integration of information; written skills; critical appraisal skills; cognitive flexibility; communication skills; conceptual skills; physical suitability/fitness to work; attainments; NHS awareness; client skills; staff skills; contraindications; experience and IT skills. However, only 20 per cent had a job description or person specification.

In line with good practice, 83 per cent of courses used quantitative rating scales for each interviewer to rate candidates, typically after each interview (79 per cent of courses). Half of all courses used aggregated ratings to decide first offer lists, 29 per cent used aggregated ratings and discussion and 21 per cent used discussion only. Courses were less likely to just use aggregated ratings when deciding reserve offers (42 per cent) and rejections (29 per cent); ratings and discussion (33 per cent and 38 per cent respectively) or discussion only (25 per cent and 33 per cent respectively) were more likely to be used.

WHO GETS ON?

The clearing house project also investigated factors associated with applicants being shortlisted for interview and selected for a training place. First, a number of factors were associated with a virtually zero likelihood of being shortlisted or offered a clinical psychology training place:

- the applicant being a current undergraduate;
- the applicant not having the British Psychological Society Graduate Basis for Registration at the time of application;
- the application form being presented very poorly;
- the academic referee rating that the applicant will not get on well with colleagues;
- the academic referee rating that the applicant will not be energetic and efficient;
- the experience-related referee stating that they would not employ the applicant again.

Second, we investigated the factors most strongly associated with being shortlisted using a logistic regression (i.e. when controlling for all factors potentially associated with being shortlisted). The best predictors of being shortlisted were:

- the applicant having the British Psychological Society Graduate Basis for Registration;
- the applicant having a better degree class;
- the applicant having started or completed a masters degree or a PhD;
- the applicant having had a greater number of psychology assistant psychologist posts or research assistant psychologist posts;
- the applicant having spent longer in paid employment;
- the applicant having worked in a greater number of different specialities;
- the academic referee giving a better overall rating of the applicant, and rating the applicant as more likely to get on well with clients;

> ➲ the experience-related referee being a clinical psychologist, giving a better overall rating of the applicant, and stating that they would employ the applicant again.

In summary, being shortlisted is associated with better academic performance, a greater duration and variety of relevant vocational experience, and better ratings from relevant referees.

Third, we used the same process to investigate which factors among shortlisted candidates were associated with eventually being offered a training place. A smaller number of factors were associated with being selected for a training place:

> ➲ the applicant having a better degree class;
> ➲ the applicant having had a greater number of psychology assistant psychologist posts or research assistant psychologist posts;
> ➲ the applicant having applied to a greater number of courses in the same region;
> ➲ the experience-related referee having written references before, and giving a better overall rating of the applicant.

Among shortlisted candidates, the ones most likely to be selected for a training place show better academic performance, a greater duration and variety of relevant vocational experience, a perceived commitment to the region where the course is located, and a better rating from a practised experience-related referee. It is worth noting that demographic factors were not associated with being shortlisted or selected to clinical psychology training, suggesting that courses are not directly discriminatory in their selection procedures.

CONCLUSIONS

For applicants to clinical psychology training, the national picture is improving all the time, with increasing numbers of training places not being matched by increases in the number of applicants. Data from the clearing house research project confirm the widely held view that applicants to clinical psychology training are largely young, white, middle-class women without significant caring responsibilities. Applicants typically have good 'A' levels or Scottish Highers and a good degree in psychology, with many applicants currently engaged in some form of postgraduate study. Vocationally, the most common posts for applicants are psychology assistant psychologist or research assistant psychologist posts, with half the applicants having been working for two years or more. Unsurprisingly, referees are generally very positive about applicants.

Courses are diverse in some of their shortlisting and selection procedures, although they all use quantitative ratings of application forms to shortlist and some type of interview as part of the selection process. Courses are also diverse in the extent to which they systematically assess the validity and reliability of their selection procedures, and many of these procedures are debatable from the standpoint of organisational psychology research evidence. However, the factors associated with shortlisting and selection to training reflect sensible priorities for courses: better academic performance, a greater duration and variety of relevant vocational experience, a perceived commitment to the region where the course is located and better ratings from relevant referees. Furthermore, the effect of selection procedures appears to be non-discriminatory in terms of the demographic characteristics of applicants, although training courses may need to work harder to attract a more diverse pool of applicants. It is also worth noting that courses are currently assuming that past academic performance and vocational experience are indicators of applicants' potential for training. Although this seems sensible, this assumption remains untested in terms of research evidence.

Finally, it is important to sound some cautionary notes for potential applicants reading this chapter. First, there were many aspects of the application process that we could not investigate, such as more subtle aspects of form presentation and applicant performance at interview. Such aspects are also clearly important in the shortlisting and selection process. Second, these data, although national in scope, are only based on one cohort of applicants to clinical psychology training. Both the characteristics of applicants and the selection procedures of the clearing house and clinical psychology training courses change every year, and different issues may well be important when you are applying. So, even if you don't fit all the factors mentioned here, don't give up, and work to maximise your chances of a successful application.

8 | Reflections from trainees

THE QUESTIONNAIRE AND THE PARTICIPANTS

Questionnaires were sent to trainee clinical psychologists on different courses across the country. The statistics that follow represent the sample of questionnaires that were returned and not the statistics for courses in general.

There are 1,244 trainees at present on courses attached to the clearing house. 118 trainees from a range of these courses completed the trainee questionnaire, 86 per cent of whom were female and 14 per cent of whom were male. 40 per cent were in their first year of training, 35 per cent were in their second year and 25 per cent were in their third year. Ages ranged from 23 to 50 with the average age for first year participants being 27, second year participants being 28 and the third year participants being 30. 92 per cent had previously worked as assistant psychologists and the range of time these people had spent working as an assistant psychologist prior to training ranged from six months to ninety-six months with the average length of time being twenty-eight months. The areas that participants worked in covered all of the areas discussed in previous chapters and also some additional specific specialisms.

REFLECTIONS ON THE POTENTIAL PROS AND CONS OF WORKING AS AN ASSISTANT PSYCHOLOGIST PRIOR TO TRAINING

The questionnaire provided an opportunity for trainees to give their views about both the benefits that can be gained and the potential problems that can arise from working as an assistant psychologist prior to training. Below are some key suggestions from trainees who previously worked as assistant psychologists. Obviously each assistant psychologist post is different but it is worth bearing these things in mind when looking for an assistant psychologist post or working within one. This expands on advice offered earlier by assistant psychologists because it relates assistant psychologist work directly to work carried out as a trainee.

Cons

⋺ *It can leave you with concerns about what to do with your career if you do not get on to a course – there is no other obvious route for using your experience as an assistant psychologist.*

⋺ *There are no guarantees that you will get on to a course as a result of doing an assistant psychologist post.*

⋺ *You can become over-familiar with styles of work or systems potentially irrelevant to clinical training and/or other professions.*

⋺ *Gaining all the relevant experience for an application, for example, both research and clinical work, is hard.*

⋺ *You can be involved in administration that does not feel directly relevant to the course.*

⋺ *You don't always work from the same theoretical stance as the course you then get a place on which can be confusing at first.*

Pros

⋺ *Gaining a good understanding of a clinical psychologist's work in the NHS and an understanding of the structure of the NHS provides a good grounding for entering this area as a trainee.*

⋺ *You get the chance to work with clients so that you then feel comfortable in doing so on your first placement.*

- ⮕ *It allows you to gain an insight into the profession and decide if it is what you definitely want to do before investing so much time and energy in applying for the courses.*
- ⮕ *If you get to work alongside trainees as an assistant psychologist you can get an idea about the kinds of work they carry out on placements and so you will know what to expect on your first placement.*
- ⮕ *It provides the opportunity to get familiar with different psychological approaches and basic clinical skills that will be used on the course.*
- ⮕ *You gain relevant experience to help get an interview and work that you can reflect on in the application form and interview.*
- ⮕ *Experience of theory and practice can make both teaching and placements easier on the course.*
- ⮕ *An opportunity to gain experience of being supervised by a clinical psychologist is useful because you will experience this again throughout training. This therefore allows you to gain some ideas about how best to utilise supervision in training.*
- ⮕ *Allows you to learn the basics regarding assessment, formulation and intervention, which you will then be able to build on in training.*
- ⮕ *It gives you a chance to build your confidence for when you start the course because things won't seem completely alien to you.*
- ⮕ *Building team-working skills and effective time-management skills as an assistant psychologist will be invaluable as a trainee.*
- ⮕ *You can have opportunities for training through conferences and workshops.*
- ⮕ *Developing research skills in a real life setting is different to undergraduate research and you will use these skills on the course.*
- ⮕ *Provides you with personal experience and therefore case examples to discuss in interview.*

> ⊖ Provides an opportunity to meet other assistant psychologists, trainees and clinical psychologists with a wealth of knowledge and experience that you can learn from.
>
> ⊖ Once you get on to a course you realise how relevant all of the experiences you had as an assistant psychologist were so don't undervalue it. Even if you think what you are doing is banal, make sure you get a real appreciation of where it fits into the wider service. You find that you also draw on each other's prior experience within your course.

REFLECTIONS ON OTHER TYPES OF WORK EXPERIENCE

Trainees also completed a section relating to other work experience that they had prior to training. There were a number of jobs that trainees had carried out as well as, or instead of, working as an assistant psychologist prior to training. Only a few participants had only worked as an assistant psychologist previously. The kinds of work that trainees had carried out related very closely to the work experience discussed earlier in Chapter 2 as alternative options to assistant psychologist posts or ways to get experience in order to gain an assistant psychologist post. This highlights once again that there are some key jobs that are commonly carried out which also provide directly relevant experience. It also highlights the fact that trainees can come from all walks of life.

A number of potential pros and cons were suggested about gaining other types of work experience in related fields. Some examples of this are listed below.

Cons

> ⊖ You can feel inadequate next to previous assistant psychologists once on training but this soon changes as the course progresses.

- If the focus of the work is not directly psychological you can forget your undergraduate teaching and then have to revisit it when working as an assistant psychologist or a trainee later.
- Some of these jobs may have been rewarding and taken up a lot of time and then get viewed as simply springboards which is frustrating.
- If this was your only experience and you did not work as an assistant psychologist as well then starting training could potentially be a culture shock. It can take time adapting to the 'psychological world' if you have not experienced it prior to training.

Pros

- It can be useful when working with other related professionals as part of multidisciplinary teams.
- It provides an opportunity to gain a greater understanding of the NHS if you work within different types of NHS services.
- You can gain a greater awareness and appreciation of other professional roles and responsibilities.
- You get a deeper understanding of the system that clients experience from different angles.
- It aids in getting a job as an assistant psychologist.
- It is good to know that everything doesn't hang on clinical psychology and it provides other options if you do not get into training.
- You can gain more client contact.
- It allows you to develop lower-level clinical skills that can be built on in future work.

ADVICE FROM TRAINEES TO THOSE ABOUT TO START ON A TRAINING COURSE

- ➔ *Go on a long holiday before the course starts so that you can start refreshed.*
- ➔ *Be prepared to feel de-skilled at the start of the course and to start questioning why you are doing it because this is very common.*
- ➔ *Be prepared to become a bit disillusioned.*
- ➔ *Read around general introductory texts but don't swamp yourself in the belief that you must know everything before you are taught it!*
- ➔ *Enjoy it. People I know who have qualified and see lots of clients each day say that they really miss being in training and that they never fully appreciated the opportunity to spend time thinking, discussing clients and studying.*
- ➔ *Time management and self-care are very important.*
- ➔ *Try to keep an open mind in teaching.*
- ➔ *Be prepared that the course won't meet all your high expectations.*
- ➔ *Build in treats for yourself – holidays, massages, shopping, etc.*
- ➔ *Make sure that you keep the course informed about how things are going for you and any needs that are not being met so that this can be dealt with.*
- ➔ *Try to meet fellow trainees before the course commences.*
- ➔ *Don't delude yourself that everyone will know more than you.*
- ➔ *It'll be a big change from being an assistant psychologist because people take you seriously and listen to what you have to say. It's all good!*
- ➔ *If you have made it on to the course remember that you deserve to be there.*
- ➔ *Don't get too carried away when you start as this will only make you burn out early on.*

- *Get outside support.*
- *Don't give up your life!*
- *Wait until you start the course before buying books and doing lots of reading.*
- *Don't get competitive — it's not a competition and peer support is essential throughout the course.*
- *Don't be afraid to ask for help.*
- *Don't hesitate to ask questions or challenge ideas.*
- *Get to know your peers as their support will be invaluable.*
- *Remember that everyone feels like a fraud.*
- *Be prepared to work very, very hard and put your personal life on hold to a large extent for three years.*
- *Be prepared for a bit of a roller coaster ride between high anxiety and stress to feeling flat and disillusioned.*
- *Look after yourself.*
- *Don't worry about it and enjoy the experience — remember that everyone else in your year is in the same boat and remember that you don't have to fill the application form in again!*
- *Keep your head down and do as much as you need to without going OTT.*
- *Keep clear boundaries about what is your time and what time you are prepared to spend working.*
- *Remember that it is a job and not a way of life.*
- *There will be a lot of 'levelling out' at the start — you will be strong in some areas where others won't be and vice versa. Remember that the course is a learning process and nobody is supposed to know everything.*
- *Get a reliable car with a radio/tape player for long journeys.*
- *Don't expect to be given all the answers — you won't get them.*
- *Enjoy the luxury of being allowed to be incompetent.*
- *Try to talk to those who have gone through it for tips.*
- *Be organised and set your own deadlines according to the pressures of work (i.e. in quiet time be getting on with work for the next deadline).*

- ➔ If the course has a buddy system make use of it to get any information you need prior to starting.
- ➔ Use training to experiment with lots of approaches until you find what works for you.
- ➔ The course will test your personal, material and financial resources so be prepared.
- ➔ Be prepared for an anticlimax when the honeymoon period wears off.

9 | The Division of Clinical Psychology and the Affiliates Group

DCP Affiliates Group

WHAT IS THE DCP?

A number of sub-systems exist under the wide umbrella of the British Psychological Society. One type of sub-system is a division. Divisions are qualification based, i.e. only those who have completed the approved training may join the division as a full member. The Division of Clinical Psychology (DCP) is the largest division in the Society, representing over 3,000 qualified clinical psychologists, and is run by elected clinical psychologists from around the UK. The main aim of the division is to promote and enhance professional practice, and the DCP does this by organising one-day events, conferences and publications. The DCP has its own monthly publication *Clinical Psychology* (previously known as *Clinical Psychology Forum*), which contains varied articles on clinical, organisational and professional aspects of clinical psychology. Information on the DCP can be found on the Society's website (www.bps.org) or in the sub-systems' notices in the monthly publication *The Psychologist*.

ASSISTANT PSYCHOLOGIST MEMBERSHIP IN THE AFFILIATES GROUP

The DCP has different levels of representation that reflect psychologists' qualifications. Those who are fully qualified are full members, i.e. clinical psychologists who have achieved a

BPS-approved postgraduate qualification in clinical psychology. Those who are in training (trainee clinical psychologists) are affiliate members, which requires that they be completing a BPS-approved postgraduate course in clinical psychology. Until recently, these were the two main levels of representation that were granted by the DCP. However, as assistant psychologist numbers continued to grow and they became significantly involved in clinical work, the DCP recognised that this particular transient group was not represented. As a result, in the year 2000 the DCP allowed assistant psychologists to become affiliate members.

Assistant psychologists can also join trade unions, with Amicus (previously MSF) taking a particular interest in assistant psychologist issues. However, until this motion was passed, assistant psychologists have not had professional representation, and their professional practices have traditionally been overseen by their supervisors. The trade union Amicus has recently conducted a survey on assistant psychologists' experiences of general working conditions including supervision. The details of the results of this study will hopefully be available at a later date.

WHY AND HOW TO BECOME AN AFFILIATE OF THE DCP?

The only criterion for becoming an affiliate member is that a chartered clinical psychologist must supervise you. Most of those affiliate members who are not trainees are employed as assistant psychologists. Some are classed as corresponding members, and are those who were eligible for affiliate membership (i.e. supervised by a clinical psychologist) but who may have changed jobs yet wish to remain attached to the DCP. Most membership runs on an annual basis and currently costs £16 per year (you must be a BPS member to join and this cost is in addition to BPS membership costs).

There are a number of benefits to being an affiliate member. First, you are able to consult the DCP over matters of professional concern and, in turn, they can raise this issue with the relevant parties. You also receive *Clinical Psychology* on a monthly basis. This, as mentioned above, is a monthly journal containing research and news articles and is very useful for keeping yourself up to date with developments in the profession. It also provides a forum for affiliates to share concerns through letters and articles highlighting particular issues. Finally, the membership can provide you with discounts on workshops, conferences and professional documents produced by the DCP.

It is useful to note that both the BPS and the DCP membership fees are tax deductible. All you need to do is contact your local tax office and tell them you are paying professional subscriptions and they will increase your tax-free allowance.

It is also useful to know that the more members there are, the more resources exist to represent assistant psychologists more effectively. The Affiliates Group is part-financed by the *Alternative Handbook* sales, and partly by a subvention it receives annually from the DCP. The *Alternative Handbook* is produced annually and contains information and advice relating to every Clin.Psy.D course. It differs from the handbook produced by the clearing house because it offers a trainee perspective to each course with information gathered from current trainees. The subvention consists of the membership fees that are paid by affiliate members.

WHERE DOES THE AFFILIATES GROUP FIT IN?

The DCP has various committees, and one of the committees is the Affiliates Group, which now represents both trainees and assistant psychologists. The committee has ten members (five trainee and five assistant psychologist) with two co-chairs (one trainee and one assistant psychologist), and other roles spread amongst the other members. Certain roles are appropriate to whether you are a trainee or an assistant psychologist. Being attached to a professional body means that members of the committee are invited to attend meetings held by other professional organisations.

The trainee members attend meetings of the Group of Trainers in Clinical Psychology (GTiCP) and the Committee on Training in Clinical Psychology (CTCP) who are heavily involved in the running and accrediting of training courses. The assistant psychologist members attend the clearing house meetings, which deal with postgraduate applications to clinical psychology training courses. They also meet with the Psychology Postgraduate Affairs Group (PsyPAG), which is a representing body for postgraduate psychologists working in various fields, for example, research psychologists.

The Affiliates Group committee also meets with Amicus, the trade union body representing clinical psychologists and other psychologists within the NHS. In addition, the co-chair members attend the full committee meetings of the DCP.

As you can see, the Affiliates Group presence on these committees allows it to keep informed of developments that may affect both trainees and assistant psychologists, and to provide a response where necessary. Affiliate members can be kept informed and up to date via the newsletter which is produced throughout the year, usually following Affiliates Group committee meetings. This is sent out to link people in assistant psychologists' groups and on training courses.

The Affiliates Group organises and runs annual conferences that are designed to appeal specifically to assistant psychologists and trainees, with discounts for DCP affiliate members. It is also currently in the process of setting up a website so watch this space!

PROFESSIONAL DEVELOPMENT ISSUES RELEVANT TO ASSISTANT PSYCHOLOGISTS

Recently, there have been developments on the job scene that could affect assistant psychologists. These are hot topics within the profession that are currently being debated. As a result it is impossible to state exactly what the future holds with regards to these issues but it is worth bearing them in mind. To find out about any significant developments that may take place in relation to such issues you could contact the Affiliates Group for further information.

The graduate primary care mental health worker

The NHS plan that came out in the summer of 2000 called for 1,000 graduate primary care mental health worker posts to be in place across England for about 2004. Initially it appeared that these posts would mainly attract psychology graduates interested in gaining experience in mental health, however, other related professions may also want to play a role in these posts. The details for these posts are still being debated and the DCP are involved in the negotiations. The idea is for the mental health workers to be given training in solution focused therapies (for example, cognitive behaviour therapy) with clients with less severe mental health problems. They will also be involved in clinical audit, and are likely to be supervised by clinical psychologists. Wales, Scotland and Northern Ireland have yet to put forward their plans for these new positions.

The associate psychologist

This is a new grade, between the traditional grades for assistant psychologist and qualified clinical psychologist, that has been piloted by an NHS trust in the Manchester area. Assistant psychologists would achieve this grade on the basis of capability, and it would allow them to increase their skills and autonomy in specific areas of practice. Supervision would still be received from a clinical psychologist. Basically, the idea behind these posts is that those with increased level of skill, e.g. higher degrees, would be acknowledged, thus raising the possibility of career development.

Training for assistant psychologists

In the last two years there have been discussions held at a number of levels about various ways of providing assistant psychologists with training to increase their skill base. These ideas range from Clin.Psy.D courses considering running programmes for assistant psychologists on day release from their jobs, to assistant psychologists proactively setting up in-house training programmes within their departments.

Similarly, there have recently been proposals for assistant psychologists to be employed on two-year contracts that would rotate through different specialities. For developments on ideas relating to training for assistant psychologists you should keep your eyes peeled for information in *Clinical Psychology*.

CONTACT US

You can contact us via the BPS offices at:

St Andrews House
48 Princess Road East
Leicester
LE1 7DR
Tel: 0116 254 9568
www.bps.org.uk

If you are interested in becoming involved with the Affiliates Group of the DCP, or even being on the committee itself then please contact us at the address above. Our annual general meeting is usually held in the summer, and people are invited to come along to see the group in action.

10 | Conclusions

The questionnaires provided the opportunity for participants to make additional comments that would be useful for putting in this publication. A lot of people wrote supportive comments, encouraging me with this idea. I found this extremely motivating. Many assistant psychologists and trainee clinical psychologists complained that nothing like this had been available to them and it would have been very useful. There were a few key points that arose from this final section of the questionnaire in terms of general advice.

The general feeling was that this can be a difficult profession to get into and that you must be certain that it is for you before attempting to get that first 'foot in the door'. It occurred to me, however, that for some people this could be an option they are simply considering and they don't want to completely commit themselves at such an early stage. In these circumstances it seems that gaining some voluntary work in a clinical psychology setting is very helpful and should assist you in making that decision. Similarly, when considering this career take into account the pros and cons so that you can make an informed decision. In order to do this it can be very beneficial to speak to as many people in the profession as possible so that you gain a fuller picture from accessing different perspectives.

Once you are sure that this profession is for you do not let anyone put you off. Many assistant psychologists have experienced people trying to discourage them by insisting the field is too competitive. Historically it certainly has been a competitive area to get into but it is becoming much less so due to the increase in training places across the country. In addition, despite the competition, the general view shared by participants with the benefit of hindsight is that it is worth pursuing if it is what you want to do. Those who do not seem to share this view tend to have been ill informed prior to making their decision.

As highlighted in previous chapters, getting an assistant psychologist post can be difficult but once you secure one, the job can be challenging and rewarding. There is obviously a lot of variability amongst posts. However, you should try to make the most of the opportunities to develop your knowledge base and skills that each post brings. It is important to remember that the work you do before getting a place on a Clin.Psy.D course is all part of the learning process and is relevant to your future career.

If you are not having any luck getting assistant psychologist jobs then remember that this is only one of the routes for gaining relevant experience. There are a lot of other jobs that you can do instead (see Chapter 2). There is also a lot of scope for doing additional courses/qualifications, which can help to strengthen your application for the Clin.Psy.D courses. It is increasingly common, though not essential, for people to have further qualifications such as masters or doctorates prior to getting on a course.

If you do not wish to continue on the clinical psychology route at all then there are other related professions you could consider. Some people who find it difficult to get a job as an assistant psychologist or a place on a clinical psychology training course, or who simply decide clinical psychology is not for them, decide to pursue other related careers. This could be, for example, in research, counselling psychology, speech and language therapy, social work, complementary therapies or health psychology, amongst others. For more information on such options you could contact the BPS.

If however you do continue down the path of clinical psychology, don't focus solely on clinical psychology but remember to put energy into the rest of your life as well. Courses are not looking for robots, but interesting, well-rounded individuals.

Most importantly when considering a career in clinical psychology, make sure that it is something that you will enjoy. If this profession is for you, then be glad that you've found it and that it brings with it a wealth of opportunities and a lifelong career.

I hope that this book has helped to guide you in the right directions and whatever you decide to do, GOOD LUCK!

Appendix 1
Assistant psychologist questionnaire

When I decided to pursue a career in clinical psychology I found it very difficult to find information and advice to help me get started. I now work as an assistant psychologist and know that we all went through similar difficulties before securing a post. As assistant psychologists we have learnt a lot about the system that I am sure we wish we knew before. I am therefore hoping to compile a book of information and advice gathered from assistant psychologists around the country that would be useful to anyone considering a career in clinical psychology. This would give us the opportunity to have our say, and I would very much appreciate it if you could complete this questionnaire with your personal experiences, views and advice, which you could then return to me in the stamped addressed envelope provided.

I will be acknowledging all contributors in the book, and hope to also include quotes from the questionnaires (I am particularly interested in including any comical anecdotes of personal experiences). If you want to remain anonymous, simply do not write your name on the questionnaire. If you have any queries please contact me on. . . .
Thank you very much for your time!!

Name: .... Age: ....
Gender: .... No. of assistant's posts: ....

Background information

1. Where did you get the information that you needed when you decided to seek a career in clinical psychology?

....
....

2. Would you have found a book like this useful and why?

....
....

3. Why did you decide to pursue a career in clinical psychology?

....
....
....
....
....

4. What is your definition of a clinical psychologist?

....
....
....
....
....
....
....
....

Work experience

1. Did you have another career before this, and if so what did you do and why did you decide to change?

....
....
....
....

2. What work experience did you get prior to getting your first assistant job and in what order?

....
....
....
....
....
....
....

3. When did you start to gain relevant experience and when would you advise somebody to start looking for experience?

....
....
....
....

4. What advice would you give regarding how and where to look for relevant work experience?

....
....
....
....

5. Please use the space below to expand on any of the above with a description of your personal experiences.

....
....
....
....
....
....
....
....
....
....
....

Applying for jobs as an assistant psychologist

1. Where do you think are the best places to look for assistant psychologist posts and when?

....
....

2. How many jobs did you apply to before you managed to secure a post?

....
....

3. How many interviews did you attend before getting the job?

....
....

4. What do you think are the most important things to look out for in the job descriptions?

....
....
....
....

5. Please use the space below to expand on any of the above and to explain in more detail about any difficulties that you have personally experienced.

....
....
....
....
....
....
....
....
....
....

Going to interviews

1. What advice could you offer to somebody preparing for an interview for an assistant psychologist job?

....
....
....
....

2. Please use the space below to describe any of your personal experiences of interviews.

....
....
....
....
....
....

Quality of experience

1. What kind of clinical work do you do in your job?

....
....
....
....

2. What kind of research work do you do in your job?

....
....
....
....

3. What other tasks do you carry out in your job?

....
....
....
....

4. How important do you think that the above experience is for an assistant psychologist and why?

....
....
....
....

Different clinical psychology specialities

1. What client group(s) do you work with?

....
....

2. Why did you choose to work with this client group?

....
....
....
....

3. What are the good and bad things about working with this client group?

....
....
....
....
....
....

4. If you have worked with other client groups in the past, which client groups have you worked with and how do they compare?

....
....
....
....

5. What advice would you give to somebody who has never worked with this client group before?

....
....
....
....

The clinical psychology courses

1. Have you applied to any clinical psychology courses, and if so, how many times?

....
....

2. Please use the space below to describe your personal experience of going through the process. This could include, for example, the amount of time it took you to complete your form, experience of going for an interview, or the amount of stress this process caused you. Please include any advice that you would offer now with the benefit of hindsight.

....
....
....
....
....
....
....
....
....
....
....
....

Finally

Please use the space on the back of this sheet to add any additional comments that you think could be useful. This may be in relation to: your personal experiences as an assistant psychologist; experiences prior to getting a job as an assistant psychologist; general advice for anyone considering a career in clinical psychology; or further details on any of the above questions or suggestions about this questionnaire and book. Please continue on a separate sheet if necessary.

Appendix 2
Trainee questionnaire

I am currently writing a book for people who are interested in a career in clinical psychology and who want to know more about getting on to training courses by gaining experience as assistant psychologists. The content of the book is largely based on information that I gathered from assistant psychologists around the country whilst working as an assistant psychologist myself. I have recently started on a clinical psychology training course and I am hoping to expand the content of the book to include additional advice from trainees on different courses based on their personal experiences. I would therefore be very grateful if you could complete the following questionnaire and return it to your course administrator.

I hope to include some quotes from completed questionnaires, which will remain anonymous. I will, however, be acknowledging all contributors in a general list. Please do not write your name on the questionnaire if you wish to remain completely anonymous.

Thank you very much for your time!!

Name: .... Age: ....
Gender: .... Course Year: ....

Did you ever work as an assistant psychologist/research assistant psychologist?   Yes   No

Section A: Please complete if you worked as an assistant psychologist or research assistant psychologist prior to training

1. How long did you work as an assistant psychologist?

....

2. Why did you choose to work as an assistant psychologist?

....

....

3. What area(s) did you work in as an assistant psychologist?

....

....

4. What benefits do you think can be gained from working as an assistant psychologist prior to training?

....

....

5. What problems do you think can arise from working as an assistant psychologist prior to training?

....

....

Section B: Please complete if you had any other work experience prior to training in addition to or instead of working as an assistant psychologist or research assistant psychologist

1. What work experience did you have prior to gaining a place on a training course?

....

....

2. What do you think the benefits were for working in this role prior to training?

....

....

3. What problems do you think can arise from working in this role prior to training?

....

....

4. If you never worked as an assistant psychologist, why was this?

....

....

Section C: To be completed by everyone

1. What general advice would you offer to somebody wishing to pursue a career in clinical psychology?

....

....

....

2. What advice would you offer to somebody applying for the training courses?

....

....

....

3. What advice would you offer to somebody going to course interviews?

....

....

....

4. What advice would you offer to somebody about to start a training course?

....

....

....

Any other comments (please continue on another sheet if necessary)

Appendix 3
Course director questionnaire

I am currently writing a book for people who are interested in a career in clinical psychology and want to know more about getting on to training courses by gaining experience as assistant psychologists. Linda Steen (Clinical Director of the Manchester Clin.Psy.D Course) is supervising this project and I have a publishing contract with Brunner-Routledge.

The content of the book is largely based on information that I gathered from assistant psychologists around the country whilst working as an assistant psychologist myself. I recently started on a clinical psychology training course and I am hoping to expand the content of the book to include additional advice from trainees and trainers on different courses based on their personal experiences. I would therefore be very grateful if you could complete the following questionnaire and return it in the stamped addressed envelope provided as soon as possible.

Professor Graham Turpin has written the foreword for the book and I am hoping also to build in a few comments from a variety of course directors within the body of the book. These shall not be presented as official and prescriptive but simply suggestions that could be useful for general guidance. I hope to include some quotes from completed questionnaires, which will remain anonymous. I will, however, be acknowledging all contributors in a general list. Please do not write your name on the questionnaire if you wish to remain completely anonymous.

Name: ....

1. What do you look for in an applicant for clinical psychology doctorate courses?

....
....
....
....

2. What do you think the benefits are from working as an assistant psychologist prior to training?

....
....
....
....

3. What do you think the potential problems are of working as an assistant psychologist prior to training?

....
....
....
....

4. What general advice would you give to someone wishing to pursue a career in clinical psychology? (Please continue any answers on the back if necessary)

....
....
....
....
....

Appendix 4
Useful addresses

THE BRITISH PSYCHOLOGICAL SOCIETY (BPS)

St Andrews House
48 Princess Road East
Leicester
LE1 7DR
Tel: 0116 254 9568
www.bps.org.uk

You can get booklets from the BPS on careers in psychology from their website. You can also contact the Division of Clinical Psychology (DCP) and the Affiliates Group of the Division of Clinical Psychology through the BPS.

THE CLEARING HOUSE

15 Hyde Terrace
Leeds
LS1 9LT
Tel: 0113 233 2737
email: chpccp@leeds.ac.uk

Application packs for clinical psychology training courses can be gained from the clearing house.

NATIONAL ASSOCIATION OF VOLUNTEER BUREAUX

You can access information from the national bureaux through their website (www.navb.org.uk). By carrying out a search using your post code and specialist interests you can access information on appropriate voluntary work in your area that you could then follow up. You can also find out how to get in touch with your local volunteer bureaux, which you could visit for more personal assistance. There are links from this website to related organisations so you should be able to access the information that you need wherever you are in the United Kingdom.

New Oxford House
16 Waterloo Street
Birmingham B2 5UG
Tel: 0121 633 4555
www.navb.org.uk

CHARITIES

Below are a few examples of appropriate national organisations that employ people in both a voluntary and paid capacity. There are many more national and local organisations working with a number of different client groups which provide similar opportunities and which can be accessed through the website mentioned above. These addresses should simply help to get you started.

MIND (NATIONAL ASSOCIATION FOR MENTAL HEALTH)

Granta House
15-19 Broadway
Stratford
London E15 4BQ
Tel: 020 8519 2122
email: info@mind.org.uk
www.mind.org.uk

MENCAP (LEADING CHARITY WORKING WITH CHILDREN AND ADULTS WITH LEARNING DISABILITIES)

Public Liaison Unit
Mencap National Centre
123 Golden Lane
London EC1Y 0RT
Tel: 020 7696 5584/5593

SANELINE (NATIONAL MENTAL HEALTH HELPLINE)

First Floor
Cityside House
40 Adler Street
London E1 1EE
Tel: 020 7375 1002
email: info@sane.org.uk

NATIONAL INSTITUTE OF HEALTH

References and bibliography

Below is a useful bibliography relating to assistant psychologist issues. Some of them are cited in the text. Nearly all of the references come from *The Psychologist* (the monthly magazine of the BPS), or from *Clinical Psychology* (previously *Clinical Psychology Forum*, the monthly journal of the DCP).

Allen, J., Finch, L., Johnson, A., Payne, M. and Scott, H. (1995) 'Assistant psychologists and clinical training: a suggestion for change', *Clinical Psychology Forum*, 75: 37.

Allez, K., Ridel, G., Tatham, M. and Warren, Z. (2000) 'Assistant Psychologists Conference', *Clinical Psychology Forum*, 145: 45-46.

Bender, M. (1996) 'The strange case of the invisible underclass: clinical psychology training and assistant psychologists', *Clinical Psychology Forum*, 87: 27-31.

Berry, M.J. (1997) 'A study of the application for clinical assistant psychologist posts in an English special hospital', *Clinical Psychology Forum*, 108: 20-23.

Birnie, J. (1997) 'Guidelines for the supervision of assistant psychologists', *Clinical Psychology*, 102: 7-9.

Black, J. and Eccles, S. (2000) 'Translating policy into practice: an initiative to implement the DCP Guidelines for employment of assistant psychologists', *Clinical Psychology Forum*, 138: 15-17.

Boyle, M., Baker, M., Bennett, E. and Charman, T. (1993) 'Selection for clinical psychology courses: a comparison of applicants from ethnic minority and majority groups to the University of East London', *Clinical Psychology Forum*, 56: 9-13.

Burton, M. and Adock, C. (1998) 'The associate psychologist: developing the graduate psychologist workforce', *Clinical Psychology Forum*, 121: 7-12.

Clare, L. (1995) 'Successful applicants for clinical training: a descriptive profile of one trainee cohort', *Clinical Psychology Forum*, 77: 31-34.

Clare, L.(1995) 'Factors influencing applicant's choice of clinical psychology courses: view of a sample of clearing house applicants', *Clinical Psychology Forum*, 81:15-18.

Cook, N. (2000) 'Choosing a clinical course', *Clinical Psychology Forum*, 144: 45-46.

Davidson, C. (1997) 'Similarities and differences between the training of clinical psychologists and counsellors', *Clinical Psychology Forum*, 101: 9-12.

Division of Clinical Psychology (1998) 'Guidelines for the employment of assistant psychologists', *Clinical Psychology Forum*, 111: 44-46.

Fleming, I. and Steen, L (eds.) (forthcoming 2003) *Supervision in Clinical Psychology*, Hove: Brunner-Routledge.

Gallagher, H. and Brosnan, N. (2001) 'Evaluating the supervision experiences of assistant psychologists', *Clinical Psychology*, 8: 39-42.

Harper, D. (1990) 'Assistant psychologists and supervision', *Clinical Psychology Forum*, 19: 33-35.

Harper, D. and Newton, T. (1988) 'Psychology technicians: their use and abuse', *Clinical Psychology Forum*, 17: 5-10.

Harvey, P. (2001) 'A thousand graduates', *Clinical Psychology Forum*, 148: 55-56.

Harvey, K. J. and Tait, A. (1999) 'A training programme for assistant psychologists', *Clinical Psychology Forum*, 25: 17-20.

Hatton, C., Gray, I. and Whittaker, A. (2000) 'Improving the selection of clinical psychologists: the clearing house research project', *Clinical Psychology Forum*, 136: 35-38.

Hayes, N. (1989) 'The skills acquired in psychology degrees', *The Psychologist*, 2 (6): 238-239.

King, S. (1998) 'Another Kind of Affiliate', *Clinical Psychology Forum*, 116: 43.

Kirkland, J. (1997) 'Positive assistant psychologists? Thoughts on the skill loss', *Clinical Psychology Forum*, 108: 15-16.

Llewelyn, S. (1998) 'Clinical psychology training', *The Psychologist*, 11 (6): 295.

Marzillier, J. and Hall, J. (eds) (1999) *What is Clinical Psychology?* (third edition), Oxford: Oxford University Press.

Miller, R. (2000) 'The NHS Plan - 1000 new graduate mental health workers in primary care', *Clinical Psychology Forum*, 143: 42-43.

Morrison, T., Linger, E. and Beck-Sanders, A. (1999) 'Undergraduate psychology placements', *Clinical Psychology Forum*, 130: 32-35.

Nadirshaw, Z. (1993) 'The implications of equal opportunities in clinical psychology training: a realist's view', *Clinical Psychology Forum*, 54: 3-6.

Nadirshaw, Z. (1993) 'Issues of race in clinical psychology training: reports from two workshop groups', *Clinical Psychology Forum*, 61: 27-28.

Nicholson, K. (1992) 'Crossing the gap: the experience of assistant psychologists', *Clinical Psychology Forum*, 42: 13-15.

Phillips, A., Hatton, C. and Gray, I. (2001) 'Which selection methods do clinical psychology courses use?', *Clinical Psychology*, 8: 19-24.

Phillips, A., Hatton, C. and Gray, I. (forthcoming) 'Factors associated with shortlisting and selection to clinical psychology training: results of a prospective national cohort study', *Journal of Occupational and Organizational Psychology*.

Phillips, A., Hatton, C., Gray, I., Baldwin, S., Burrell-Hodgson, G., Cox, M., Hoy, J., McCormick, R., Rockliffe, C. and Wilson, J. (2001) 'Core competencies in clinical psychology: a view from trainees', *Clinical Psychology*, 1: 27-32.

Rezin, V. and Tucker, C. (1998) 'The uses and abuses of assistant psychologists', *Clinical Psychology Forum*, 115: 37-48.

Roth, T. (1998) 'Getting on clinical training courses', *The Psychologist*, 11 (12): 589-592.

Roth, T. and Leiper, R. (1995) 'Selecting for clinical training', *The Psychologist*, 8: 25-28.

Scott, J. and Glissov, P. (1998) 'Professional development of assistant psychologists', *The Psychologist*, 11 (11): 517-518.

Tattershall, E. et al. (1997) 'Lost in the mist: the perspective of four assistant psychologists', *Clinical Psychology Forum*, 105: 19-21.

Taylor, A. (1999) 'Supervision experiences of assistant psychologists', *Clinical Psychology Forum*, 125: 26-28.

Webb, Z. and Dodd, K. (2001) 'Beyond the guidelines for employment of assistant psychologists: establishing an appraisal system to help assistant psychologists reflect on their future careers', *Clinical Psychology*, 9: 37-40.

Whomsley, S. (1998) 'Trainee Forum: the assistant psychologists' room', *Clinical Psychology Forum*, 112: 47-48.

Williams, W. (2001) 'Relevant experience', *The Psychologist*, 14 (4): 188-189.

UNIVERSITY OF MICHIGAN

3 9015 05157 4658